MY FAITH STILL HOLDS

COMPILED BY JOYCE WILLIAMS

Beacon Hill Press of Kansas City
Kansas City, Missouri

Printed in the
United States of America

Cover Design: Ted Ferguson

Library of Congress Cataloging-in-Publication Data

My faith still holds / compiled by Joyce Williams.
    p. cm.
  ISBN 0-8341-2078-X (pbk.)
 1. Christian women—Religious life. I. Williams, Joyce, 1944- II. Title
  BV4527.M89 2003
  277.3'083'0922—dc22

2003017689

10 9 8 7 6 5 4 3

CONTENTS

FOREWORD
BELIEVING GOD

Beth Moore

My resistance to the faith principle given to us by Jesus—
"According to your faith will it be done to you" (Matt. 9:29)—was
primarily the result of spiritual laziness. To be perfectly honest,
for years I taught and walked believing in God. It has just been in
recent times that I have truly grasped that we must not only
believe *in* God—but also *believe* God. Fully implementing this
principle of faith has changed my life.

Believing God can really be work at times! When external
evidences scream to the contrary, we have to exert volitional
muscle. Deciding to believe God's Word over our circumstances
can be a tremendous exercise of the will. I'll just go ahead and
say it: the great adventure of faith is not for the languid, but if He
can raise the dead, He can surely enliven the lazy! We have been
called to a present, active walk of faith, not a park and ride. Christ
is attracted to a faith that's up-to-date.

The walk of faith assumes a walk with God. Faith cannot walk
alone. Faith on its own changes nothing. In fact, it cannot even
exist independently. Faith's very essence is dependency. For faith
to have life, it must find a powerful object in which to be placed
or a powerful Person by whom to walk.

It's important for us to remember that faith on its own does
nothing to heal. Throughout the Bible we read that the
beneficiaries' faith in Christ is what resulted in their healing.
When the two blind men asked Jesus for mercy in Matt. 9:27-30,
He responded by asking them, "Do you believe that I am able to
do this?" Their reply was simply "Yes, Lord." In answer to their

faith Jesus "touched their eyes and said, 'According to your faith will it be done to you'; and their sight was restored."

That promise is still true today. We serve the same God. He has much He wants to do and say in our generation. Our Father is ready and willing to stretch forth His mighty hand in our lives in manifold ways.

That's not to say that God will always answer our prayers according to our requests. Sometimes it doesn't seem fair. We pray, fast, trust, and believe that His touch will come. He appears to turn His back on us, and our prayers seem to bounce off the ceiling. Regardless of how much faith we have and how much we believe in God, sometimes His answer is no.

That's when we must acknowledge that our Father says, "My thoughts are not your thoughts, neither are your ways my ways" (Isa. 55:8). Through tenaciously believing His promises, we can still bow on our knees and trust Him even when He does not seem to be responding. Many times the greatest miracle may be when He gives us the grace to accept His no and then allow Him to build on that foundation of faith. These are times when the most vital dimension of believing God is believing He *is* God.

Just as mysteriously, sometimes our God acts when He sees little or no faith at all just to show us His grace and sovereignty. According to the Gospels, however, one of Christ's most common methods of operation is responding to our faith.

When we come to the point of believing Him and responding simply, *Yes, Lord*, He will reward us according to our faith. His answers are not always what we would desire them to be. But because we *believe* Him we can *trust* Him.

This book is filled with stories of faith that are shared by godly women from around the world. Each one of them has embraced the principle that Jesus taught, "According to your faith will it be done to you." As a result, they have witnessed God's answers through all kinds of life experiences.

Through simple faith in the Lord, you can trust Him, and He

will do the same in your life today. Remember: the foundation of your faith is your utter dependency upon Him—regardless of what happens in your life. Faith is the primary means by which you place your hand in the outstretched hand of God and join Him. Then, regardless of where your path may take you, you can count on Him to lead and guide you throughout the days of your life and to finally lead you home.

🖌 **Beth Moore** *is an internationally acclaimed speaker, Bible teacher, and writer. Her speaking engagements carry her to all corners of the United States and around the world. Beth and her husband, Keith, have two daughters and live in Houston, Texas. Her "Believing God" on-line Bible study can be found at www.BelievingGod.com. Copyright 2002 LifeWay Christian Resources. Used by permission.*

PREFACE
THE UNSEEN

It is when we are hurting the most that we run to God. We recognize that we are powerless and that He is powerful. We pray and we see Him more clearly because we're desperately looking for Him.

And in our looking for Him, we find Him to be more loving and faithful than we've seen Him before, perhaps because we're looking for Him so intently. That is always God's purpose: To use whatever means He sees fit to bring us to a closer relationship with Him, to create in us a faith that will give us the strength to keep holding on to hope—not a flimsy wishing or a hope that everything will be fixed in this life but genuine biblical hope that one day what is unseen will be seen. This faith is confidence in an eternal future in which God sets everything right.

From *Holding onto Hope,* Nancy Guthrie (Wheaton, Illinois: Tyndale House Publishers, Inc., 2002). Used by permission.

Nancy Guthrie has worked in Christian publishing for 18 years, handling special editorial projects and media relations for well-known Christian communicators as well as for CBA. She has been active in leadership for Bible Study Fellowship.

Section 1

Do not look forward to

what may happen tomorrow.

The same everlasting Father

who cares for you today

will care for you

tomorrow and every day.

—Francis de Sales

1 ⚜ Laura Bush

A FIRST LADY OF FAITH

In the recent past it has been a blessing to know that those who reside in the White House, the chief residence of the United States president and his family in Washington, D.C., possess deep and abiding faith in God. In September 2001 first lady Laura Bush comforted the nation with her words of hope as she spoke at a memorial service in Pennsylvania following the terrorist attacks in New York City, in Washington, D.C., and on an airliner over southern Pennsylvania.

This has been a week of loss and heartache of a kind none of us could have ever imagined. What happened in New York City, in Washington, and here in Pennsylvania caused deep suffering across our country.

We are still grieving as details become known—and especially as we learn the names of the lost, the story of their deaths, and the story of each of their lives. All of us as Americans share in this grief.

The burden is greatest, however, for the families—like those of you who are with us today. America is learning the names, but you know the people. And you are the ones they thought of in the last moments of life—even in those horrible moments. They were not truly alone, because your love was with them.

And I want each of you to know today that you are not alone. We cannot ease the pain, but this country stands by you. We will always remember what happened that day and to whom it happened.

I know many of you have felt very directly the compassion of

America, both in the communities where you live and in this community where we meet. And on behalf of my husband and the nation, I want to thank every person who has reached out to you with words of sympathy and acts of kindness.

In hours like this, we learn that our faith is an active faith, that we are called to serve and to care for one another and to bring hope and comfort where there is despair and sorrow.

All of this is the work of the living. And as it begins, however long it lasts, we will always hold close to the memory of those who have been taken from you and from us.

One of last Thursday's victims, in his final message to his family, said that he loved them and would see them again. That brave man was a witness for the greatest hope of all—and that hope unites us now. You grieve today, and the hurt will not soon go away. But that hope is real, and it is forever, just as the love you shared with your loved ones is forever.

On May 2, 2002, Mrs. Bush expressed her faith in God as she introduced her husband on the National Day of Prayer.

I would like to share with you a psalm that has special meaning in my life and speaks volumes to many of us during difficult times.

Psalm 46

God is our refuge and strength, an ever-present help in trouble.

Therefore we will not fear, though the earth give way and the mountains fall into the heart of the sea,

though its waters roar and foam and the mountains quake with their surging. . . .

There is a river whose streams make glad the city of God, the holy place where the Most High dwells.

God is within her, she will not fall; God will help her at break of day.

Laura Bush

Nations are in uproar, kingdoms fall; he lifts his voice, the earth melts.

The LORD Almighty is with us; the God of Jacob is our fortress. . . .

Come and see the works of the LORD, the desolations he has brought on the earth.

He makes wars cease to the ends of the earth; he breaks the bow and shatters the spear, he burns the shields with fire.

"Be still and know that I am God; I will be exalted among the nations, I will be exalted in the earth."

The LORD Almighty is with us; the God of Jacob is our fortress.

These words give us hope and confidence by reminding us of God's infinite strength. My husband and I find strength in the Word of the Lord, and we realize the power that prayer has in our lives.

I am truly blessed to be married to a man who is strong enough to bear great burdens and humble enough to ask God for help.

America can be grateful to God for brave leaders of faith who stand tall before our nation when our world is in turmoil.

The First Lady's comments can be found in their entirety at www.whitehouse.gov.

Laura Bush

2 Condoleezza Rice

NATIONAL PRAYER BREAKFAST

The following is excerpted from Condoleezza Rice's remarks at the National Prayer Breakfast in Washington, D.C., on February 6, 2003.

I am the daughter, the granddaughter, and indeed the niece of ordained Presbyterian ministers. Sundays in my family meant church. It was the center of our lives. In segregated Black Birmingham of the late 1950s and early 1960s, the church was not just a place of worship—it was the social and civic center of our community.

Throughout my life I have never doubted the existence of God, but like most people, I have had some ups and downs in practicing my faith. After I moved to California in 1981 to join the faculty at Stanford, there were a lot of years when I was not attending church regularly. I was traveling a great deal, always in a different time zone, and going to church too often fell by the wayside.

Then something happened that I will always remember. One Sunday morning I was approached at the supermarket by a man buying some things for his church picnic. He asked me, "Do you play the piano by any chance?"

I said, "Yes."

And he said his congregation was looking for someone to play the piano at their church. It was a small African-American church in the center of Palo Alto, and I started playing there every Sunday. And I thought to myself, *My goodness! God has a long reach—*

all the way to a Lucky's Supermarket in the spice section on a Sunday morning!

The only problem was, it was a Baptist church, and I don't play gospel very well, unlike our great attorney general, John Ashcroft. I play Brahms. At this church the minister would start with a song, and the musicians had to pick it up. I had no idea what I was doing. So I called my mother, who had played for Baptist churches, to ask her for advice. She said, "Honey, just play in C, and they'll come back to you." And that's true. If you play in C, the foundational key in music, people will come back. Perhaps God plays in C, and that's why we always seem to find our way back to Him, sometimes in spite of ourselves.

Looking back on the years since I found my way back, it is hard for me to imagine my life without a strong and active faith. Faith is what gives me comfort, humility, and hope—even through the darkest hours. Like many people, here and abroad, I have turned to God and prayer more and more this past year and a half, including this past Saturday morning. Terror and tragedy have made us more aware of our vulnerability and our own mortality. We are living through a time of testing and consequence—and praying that our wisdom and will are equal to the work before us. And it is at times like these that we are reminded of a paradox—that it is a privilege to struggle. A privilege to struggle for what is right and true. A privilege to struggle for freedom over tyranny. A privilege even to struggle with the most difficult and profound moral choices.

American slaves used to sing, "Nobody knows the trouble I've seen—glory hallelujah!" Growing up, I would often wonder at the seeming contradiction contained in this line. But as I grew older, I came to learn that there is no contradiction at all.

I believe this same message is found in the Bible in Rom. 5, where we are told to "[boast] in our sufferings, knowing that suffering produces endurance, and endurance produces character, and character produces hope, and hope does not disappoint us, because God's love has been poured into our hearts through the Holy Spirit which has been given to us" (NRSV).

For me, this message has two lessons.

First, there is the lesson that only through struggle do we realize the depths of our resilience and understand that the hardest of blows can be survived and overcome. Too often when all is well, we slip into the false joy and satisfaction of the material and a complacent pride and faith in ourselves. Yet it is through struggle that we find redemption and self-knowledge. In this sense it is a privilege to struggle, because it frees one from the idea that the human spirit is fragile, like a house of cards, or that human strength is fleeting.

We see this theme is illustrated in sacred texts the world over. In the Book of Job, God tests Job's faith by taking from him everything that he cherishes—his wealth, his health, and his family. Early in his trials, one of Job's friends counsels him to be patient, saying, "Behold, happy is the man whom God correcteth: therefore despise not thou the chastening of the Almighty: for he maketh sore, and bindeth up: he woundeth, and his hands make whole. . . . In famine he shall redeem thee from death: and in war from the power of the sword. . . . And thou shalt know that thy tabernacle shall be in peace" (Job 5:17-18, 20, 24, KJV). In the end, Job's sufferings strengthen his faith, and, we are told, he is rewarded with "twice as much as he had before" (42:10, KJV), and he lived 140 years until he was "old and full of days" (v. 17, KJV). We learn in times of personal struggle—in the loss of a loved one, in illness, or in turmoil—that there is a peace that passeth understanding. When our intellect is unequal to the task—the spirit takes over, finding that peace in the midst of pain is the true fulfillment of our humanity.

Struggle doesn't just strengthen us to survive hard times—it is also the key foundation for true optimism and accomplishment. Indeed, personal achievement without struggle somehow feels incomplete and hollow. It is true, too, for humankind—because

 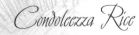

nothing of lasting value has ever been achieved without sacrifice.

There is a second, more important, lesson to be learned from struggle and suffering. It is that we can use the strength it gives us for the good of others. Nothing good is born of personal struggle if it is used to fuel one's sense of entitlement, or superiority to those who we perceive to have struggled less than we. Everyone in this room has been blessed, and I am sure we all know that it is dangerous to think about the hand that one has been dealt relative to others if it ends in questioning why someone else has more. It is, on the other hand, sobering and humbling to think about one's blessings and to ask why you have been given so much when others have so little.

Our goal must not be to get through a struggle so that others can congratulate us on our resilience, nor is it to dwell on struggle as a badge of honor.

Perhaps this is why in describing his personal struggle, the apostle Paul felt it necessary to say to the Philippians, "Forgetting those things which are behind and reaching forward to those things which are ahead, I press toward the goal for the prize of the upward call of God in Christ Jesus" (Phil. 3:13-14, NKJV).

But to direct the energies from our struggles toward the good of others, we must first let go of the pain and the bad memories and the sense of unfairness—of "Why me?"—that inevitably accompany deep personal turmoil.

I believe this lesson applies not only to individuals but also to nations. America emerged from the losses of September 11 as a nation that is not only stronger but hopefully better and more generous as well. Tragedy made us appreciate our freedom more—and to be more conscious of the fact that God gives all people everywhere the right to be free. It made us more thankful for our own prosperity, for life, and health—and more aware that all people everywhere deserve the opportunity to build a better future.

It prompted us to cultivate what the president has called "the habit of service" to others so that the "gathering momentum

Condoleezza Rice   17

of millions of acts of kindness" may bring hope to people in desperate need. And perhaps most important, September 11 reminded us of our heritage as a tolerant nation; one that welcomes people of all faiths, or no faith at all.

Now, as our nation once again deals with great loss, with fears and uncertainties, let us once again recommit ourselves to those values that define us. Let us renew our quest for understanding the natural world and all the heavens, which God has made. Let us renew our commitment to standing for life and liberty and peace for all people. Let us renew our commitment to working with all nations to conquer want and hunger and disease in every corner of the globe. Let us accept our responsibility to defend the freedom that we are so privileged to enjoy.

If terror and tragedy spur us to rediscover and strengthen these commitments, then we can truly say that some good has come from great loss. And in all the trials that may lie ahead, we will carry these commitments close to our heart so we may leave a better world for those who follow. This is our prayer for our nation and our people. This is our prayer for all nations and all peoples. *Lord, hear our prayer.*

🌾 **Condoleezza Rice *serves as national security adviser to United States President George W. Bush. For six years she was Stanford University's provost and was professor of political science.***

Dr. Rice's comments can be found in their entirety at www.whitehouse.gov.

3 ⚜ Karyn Frist

WHITE PICKET FENCE

When I was a child I often climbed to the top of our old barn near our home in west Texas and looked out on the horizon and dreamed. "Fantasized" might be the more accurate word. I fantasized about my great-grandmother who traveled with her family in a covered wagon from Missouri to that very spot. She lived in a half dugout while the main house and barn were being built. I wondered about her children, her relationship with her husband, her faith. What bravery it took to leave her secure home and venture to the Wild West to start a new life! My great-grandmother's faith began a legacy that my grandmother—a baby in that covered wagon—passed on to me.

I dreamed about the life I would live when I grew up—and I prayed. I remember climbing the wobbly wooden stairs to the hayloft, where I felt closest to God. In my mind, the hayloft was God's basement. I especially loved being up in the loft as the sun dropped below the earth and the bright stars began to pop out of the darkening sky. I spent hours there planning my life.

Twenty years later, almost all those plans had been accomplished. I was married to a man who almost exactly matched my dreams—even to his physical appearance. I had three healthy children, a dog, and flower boxes. Just about everything except the white picket fence was mine. My husband, Bill, had completed years of medical training that necessitated his being away from home, and we were finally settling down to what I thought would be the rest of my life. Bill's demanding schedule during medical school hadn't allowed us much time to devote to nurturing our relationship, and this was going to be the time. I prayed about it often, even falling on my knees and crying to God.

I wasn't prepared for Bill's announcement the day he came home with the news that he was going to run for the U.S. Senate from Tennessee. He had mentioned to me often that he might be interested in entering public service, but I never thought he would actually run for office or that I would be the "adoring wife with the admiring gaze." This was *not* part of my dream 20 years earlier in that hayloft.

Nevertheless, before I knew it, the campaign was off and running. Suddenly people were telling me what to do, what not to do, and what to wear. I *tried* to get involved, but this wasn't my plan! My plan was to use this time for us—to strengthen our relationship, maybe have our fourth child, and possibly build a white picket fence *together*.

The primary campaign only lasted 10 months, but it seemed like an eternity. I suppose I remained resistant to the whole idea. Before I knew it, Bill had won the primary and jumped in with even more intensity to the general election campaign.

The night before the general election, Bill and I decided to go to church in Nashville. I can't remember why we chose this particular church—we had never been there before.

As I sat in the sanctuary singing hymns, praying, and listening to the minister, I sensed something much greater was happening. A presence so strong filled the room. It filled my mind, my body, my heart, my thoughts, and my prayers. I know it was God and the Holy Spirit. The feeling was so strong that I could almost *see* Christ's presence. From that moment, I knew Bill was going to win. I knew this was God's plan—not my plan—and I knew the white picket fence would have to wait. I remember thinking that it was too bad I had spent months fighting God's plan. So much for my hayloft dreams.

In December 2002 Bill and I decided to scale back on our commitments and spend more time as a family. But a series of

unfortunate events occurred in the Senate that resulted in Bill's being asked by his colleagues to become majority leader of the United States Senate. In a week's time, our entire lives changed abruptly. Bill wrestled with the decision, and so did I. One night we both woke up at the same time, and in the silent dark bedroom Bill said, "I don't know what to do." We both felt God in the room that night. We knew once again we were to follow, even though we didn't understand the direction He was leading us.

On the night of December 22, 2002, we went back to the church in Nashville, the same one we had attended before the two previous elections. At the end of the service, the minister asked Bill and me to come forward and kneel at the altar while the congregation circled around and prayed for us. The following day Bill was elected by his fellow senators to become the 18th majority leader of the United States Senate.

In the years following his first campaign, Bill and I have learned to trust in the words of Prov. 16:9—"In his heart a man plans his course, but the Lord determines his steps." I still dream my dreams, but I never want to get so caught up in my own dreams that I'm not open to following God's plan.

🌿 **Karen Frist** *has worked to create a home of faith for her husband, Senate Majority Leader Bill Frist, and their three sons. Her experiences as a school teacher and mother have shaped her advocacy for children's issues including literacy, children's health, child abuse, and Christian education. She supports the arts through her work on the Congressional Board of the National Museum of Women in the Arts, the Ford Theater Board of Trustees, and the Meridian International Center Boards.*

4 — Joyce Williams

HAZEL MABE'S HEAVENLY TREASURE

No one ever guessed that the quiet little lady who lived so frugally would some day leave over $1 million for world evangelism. Hazel Mabe was a quiet, unprepossessing lady who lived quite modestly. Her life demonstrated that her priorities were in divine order.

Her faith in God was obvious.

For more than 50 years she drove to church Sunday after Sunday in her aging sedan and slipped unobtrusively into a back pew at First Church of the Nazarene in Roanoke, Virginia. I remember her ready smile and her expression of wide-eyed wonder.

As a little girl I sat behind Hazel Mabe in church one Sunday morning. I was totally fascinated by the beauty of the fawn-colored velvet hat perched precisely on her head. I was especially intrigued with the colorful feather tucked into its band. Although I should have been listening to the preacher's message, I must confess that I was absorbed with the idea of stroking that soft velvet and smoothing that feathery plume.

Although she was very quiet and ladylike, Hazel was strongly opinionated about some subjects. She never hesitated to express her thoughts on issues in which she firmly believed. Because of her modesty, very few people knew that she had attended Asbury College. She had keen insight and perception—and people listened when she talked.

Although she chose to live in an aging two-story brick house on a busy corner, there's no doubt now that she could have moved out to a quieter, more affluent neighborhood. But she was perfectly content to stay right where she was and drive her old car.

You see, Hazel Mabe had her heart set on property that was out of this world. Her investment strategy was to store up treasures in a place where moths and rust could not destroy them and where thieves could not break in and steal (Matt. 6:20). With that in mind, when she finalized her estate plans, she indicated her heart's desire to leave her assets to the church to be used for the expansion of the Kingdom. She wanted her faith to be perpetuated throughout the world.

Late Sunday evening, January 30, 1999, Wayne Dunman stopped by his office on his way home from church. Since his office was across the street from where Hazel lived, he and his wife, Becky, had gotten into the habit of checking on Hazel. When he noticed that her drapes were still open and the lights still burning brightly, he immediately realized that something was wrong. He walked over to her house and knocked on the door. When there was no answer. Wayne peeked in the window. To his dismay, he saw her sitting slumped in her comfortable old chair. She had passed away.

How fitting to realize that on that Lord's Day Hazel had sat down for a nap and never awakened! It was as though the Father said, *Come home, dear child. It's time for you to join your treasures. I have beautiful riches and wealth beyond measure to show you.*

When her will was probated, properties liquidated, and her estate settled, a check in the amount of $1,214,000 was presented to Louie Bustle in a special service on May 6, 2001. She had stipulated that those funds be used by the Department of World Mission of the Church of the Nazarene to take the gospel around the world—especially to the poorest of the poor. Because of Hazel Mabe's heavenly investments, countless numbers will hear the gospel.

So many times we are tempted to collect feathers for our caps and garnish our works with grandiose gestures. Through her example, Hazel Mabe is still teaching us life lessons: don't store up treasures here. Invest them so that dividends will compound for eternity. Live humbly, stand for what's right, and deposit your assets in the eternal vaults of heaven.

Hazel Mabe's velvety, feathered hat is long gone. Her reward is the crown given to her by her precious Savior.

🌾 **Joyce Williams,** *the compiler of this book, and her husband, Gene, are founding directors of Shepherds' Fold Ministries, a ministry of encouragement to pastors and their families. They have worked on special assignments for the Billy Graham Evangelistic Association. They live in Wichita, Kansas.*

5   *Joyce Williams*

BEATRICE AGNEW'S INVESTMENTS

I was going to college! My lifelong dream was being fulfilled. Daddy had sold the sewing machine, and that money, along with scholarships, would cover the first quarter's tuition. I was so excited.

Daddy had lived with the hope that one of the females in our family would take up sewing and save him lots of money. His lack of education prevented him from getting a well-paid job, so he worked at any job he could get in order to support us. One of his jobs was painting houses. When a man he worked for was unable to pay him in cash for painting his house, Daddy took an almost-new Singer sewing machine as payment. The problem was that none of us had the talent or the patience to even make it through the free lessons Singer offered with the machine.

One of my greatest concerns about going to college was my wardrobe. I had very few clothes, and we had very limited resources. I didn't share my need with anyone, but one day Beatrice Agnew called. She and her husband were lifelong members of our church, and she was a master seamstress. We had been next-door neighbors in Roanoke, Virginia, when I was a child. Her granddaughter Connie and I were close friends, and since my grandmothers were both in heaven, I had grown to love her as an adopted grandma. I spent many afternoons in her sewing room right off her kitchen watching her work her magic with that machine. Over the years she had crafted beautiful clothes for many people.

One day she called and she said, "Joyce, I hear you're going to get to go to college. Could you come by to see me? I have some fabric, and I'd like to make some dresses for you to take with you."

Tears welled up in my eyes, and I replied, "I'll be over in a little while." She took my measurements. I still remember her comforting touch as she carefully made sure of the dimensions. She made two beautiful dresses that she brought to church the Sunday before I left for college.

To this day I remember the way those dresses felt and looked. They were simple shirtwaists, but to me they were garments of splendor—because they had been made with love.

Those dresses were expressions of Mrs. Agnew's faith in God. You see, He had blessed her with a gift that she shared generously. I remember thinking that she was sewing for Jesus.

I wasn't the only one she blessed with her sewing. Many others were on the receiving end of her kind generosity. However, her expression of faith was also a reflection of confidence in me. In those first lonely weeks, homesick and far away from family and friends, every time I wore those dresses I was wrapped in love from home.

And I must say that every stitch was cherished as an investment in God's plan for my life.

Joyce Williams

6   Glenda Parrish

LEGACY OF FAITH

The first grade teacher stood with her finger pointed at the chalkboard. As she instructed the class on the alphabet, her voice droned on and on, and the sagging skin under her arm shook. I didn't really want to be in school anyway, and before long the whole spectacle made my stomach ache.

When I could bear it no more, I asked to go to the nurse's office. There I called my grandparents to come rescue me. As I waited, the thought of my grandfather pulling up to the school's front door in his yellow Checker taxicab eased my stomach pains. I knew that he would cheerfully welcome me into the car and take me to my grandmother, Beatrice Agnew. Grandma would have a plate of freshly fried potato chips waiting for me. Then I would settle in for a loving chat beside the sewing machine where she so diligently worked.

Grandma's sewing machine sat in front of double windows with a chair beside it. We talked for hours about whatever was on her mind or mine. During those sessions she taught me about love and hard work and—even more important—faith in Jesus Christ. She made the fact that Jesus shed His blood for me understandable and real to my young mind. She told me that Jesus loved me uniquely and that I would live with Him forever if I gave my life to Him.

Along with her words, my grandmother *demonstrated* a personal relationship with Christ. It was the source of her kindness, which repeatedly prompted her to give up her own wants and desires in the interest of helping others—especially her children and grandchildren.

How grateful to God I am for giving me such an example of faith to follow! As a mother myself, I pray often that my own four children and then my grandchildren will find something in my life to encourage them in their walk with Christ.

As believers we have the great privilege and responsibility of communicating to those around us that God's Son Jesus came, died on the Cross for our sins, and rose from the grave, and that all who trust Him will have eternal life—just as my grandmother showed me.

 **Glenda Parrish** *and her husband, Preston, have four children. He serves as executive vice president of the Billy Graham Evangelistic Association. They reside in Charlotte, North Carolina.*

7 ❦ Thelma Wells

FAITH ENOUGH TO FLY

I've been told that the bumblebee isn't built for flying. Nevertheless, day after day it spreads its inadequate wings and lifts its cumbersome body into flight. Thank God for bumblebees! God has proven over and over that if we trust and believe in Him, we can soar to heights that seem impossible. We can defy the odds if we allow Him to accomplish His plan for our lives.

When I was a chubby little girl being raised by my great-grandparents, people sometimes looked at me, an illegitimate little black girl, and said, "She'll never amount to anything." But in spite of those obstacles, God has proven His lavish love for me over and over. He has enabled me to overcome my circumstances and to fly high in faith.

My mother was practically a child herself when I was born in the back room of her parents' home. She scribbled "Baby Girl Morris" on my birth certificate. Although she had been partially paralyzed by a stroke a few hours after her own birth, her will was indomitable. Not long after I came along, we went to live in the servants' quarters of a rich white family in Dallas.

When I was about two years old, my mother and I became very sick, and she lost her job. She moved to a tent with my half-sister, Sarah. Then she took me to live with my great-grandparents, Grannie and Daddy Harrell, in their tiny back-alley garage apartment. My mother told Grannie that she would let her keep me but that she was not giving me to her. Several years later my great-grandparents and I "moved up" when we went to the projects to live. We didn't have much in the way of material things, but our tiny home on that back alley was filled with love, and I knew that was where I belonged.

I was also very close to my grandfather, Daddy Lawrence. Growing up under the "Jim Crow" laws of the South, he taught me to believe that prejudice and segregation would someday end. When we went to the Majestic Theater, I remember walking with him through the side doors marked "Colored Only." They were far removed from the main entrance, and I held tightly to his hand. He whispered, "It won't always be like this, child. The day will come when you can go anywhere and sit wherever you want to sit."

In the face of prejudice, he taught me to show respect—even when white patrons yelled up into the "buzzard roost" where we sat, "Shut up, niggers! You're too loud!" Daddy Lawrence's faith in God enabled him to believe things would change. Years later I was called to the Majestic Theater to enjoy a production along with many others who represented almost all the races on earth. I wish Daddy Lawrence could have been there—sitting right down front—to enjoy the changes he always believed would happen.

Growing up in the neighborhood, I was surrounded by godly, caring people who nurtured and protected me. St. John Missionary Baptist Church was a vital part of my life. As a young child I committed myself to Jesus Christ. One of my favorite pastimes after school was to "play church." Daddy Harrell and I belted out old songs and prayed long-winded prayers in our make-believe church in the parlor of our tiny apartment. Those lyrics and prayers taught me to believe that all things are possible through faith in Jesus Christ.

I witnessed firsthand that if we believe in and rely on Him, God takes care of His people. He loves us with a lavish love! Today I tell audiences, "If God had a weakness, that weakness would be in loving His children too much. He lavishes His love on us and just keeps on giving to us. The closest thing that compares

with God's unconditional love is a mother's love." I always tell crowds, "You can mess with my money and maybe even my honey. But don't mess with my children!" And that's how our Heavenly Father feels about us too. His lavish love gives us the faith to know that He will take care of us everywhere we go. He gives us more grace—unmerited favor. I tell you—it's a lot better to have God's favor than money.

Prejudice against me didn't come just from white people. My grandmother Dot, whom I called "Mother Dot," resented me too. She was light-skinned, and when I visited her and Daddy Lawrence, it was obvious that my dark skin was a burden to her. When Daddy Lawrence wasn't there, without a word she would lead me to a tiny closet in the front bedroom. She made me stay in there for hours while she ironed white people's clothes in the front parlor. I huddled in a tight ball in that closet that smelled of mothballs and old wool. Holding tight to my blanket, I would finally go to sleep. When my grandfather discovered what she was doing, he limited my time alone with Mother Dot.

The love of Grannie and Daddy Harrell, Daddy Lawrence, and so many other friends, neighbors, and church members, along with my faith in God, enabled me to overcome all these obstacles. I did well in school and graduated with honors. Life was great. I won many awards and dated a wonderful young man named George Wells, whom I had met at church when I was 14 years old.

Then I ran headfirst into a harsh wall of prejudice when I tried to enroll in the city's finest secretarial school. I was crushed when the registrar told me, "We don't accept niggers in this school." All my way home on the streetcar that day I fought to control the anger that churned inside. That humiliation and unfairness took me right back to the darkness of the tiny closet in Mother Dot's bedroom.

When I got home, Grannie saw how devastated I was. She wrapped her arms around me and wiped away my tears. Then she said, "Don't worry, child. If you want to go to college, God will work it out." Then I understood that I had a choice: I could dwell on my anger and accept the fact that I couldn't fly. Or, like the bumblebee, I could lean on my faith in God and do the impossible. I made the right choice, because I knew that God would see me through. And has He ever!

I've learned that accomplishing goals requires God's help along with the voluntary sacrifice of many people. Through the great sacrifices of Grannie and the generosity of her employer, I graduated from college with a degree in education. George Wells and I got married during my second year of college, and he stood by me. Our three children bless our lives.

Through the years I've enjoyed many great triumphs and suffered some heartaches. God blessed George's business and rewarded our faith. He opened doors for me beyond my wildest imagination. I found myself giving motivational talks across the country and around the world. Our faith in God was the foundation of our lives. When we needed a house for our growing family, God gave us just what we needed. My aunt and uncle sold their place to us for half price. Financial reverses came, but God still provided for us and saw us through.

Looking back over the years of prejudice, closets, and impossibilities, I thank God that He gave me the faith to believe that through Him I could soar above all obstacles. Like that chubby little bumblebee that wasn't made for flying, we *can* overcome all the odds. God will take us to heights we never imagined. He has surely done that for me.

Hold tightly to your faith. In Christ you can fly against incredible odds—just like the bumblebee.

🐝 **Thelma Wells** *is an author, professor, and singer. She speaks at Women of Faith gatherings throughout North America and is president of A Woman of God Ministries. She and her husband, George, live in Dallas.*

Thelma Wells

8 ❧ Barbara Johnson

FAITH TO LET GO

All of us have things we tend to hold tightly in white-knuckled fists. When we learn to truly release those sorrows, prodigal children, heartaches, regrets, and failures from our determined clutches, we can truly experience inner peace and joy. It takes faith in God to genuinely let go of the painful passages of our lives.

One of the things that has really helped me to get through the agonizing aspects of life is humor. Over the years, I've received tons of mail to fill my "joy room." They have included little snippets of encouragement and instruction like the following:

- Never take a laxative and a sleeping pill the same night.
- Say yes when you want to say no.
- Try squeezing the toothpaste tube from the bottom.
- Do a kind deed anonymously.
- Try to understand your relatives.
- Leave a funny card for your mail carrier.
- Laugh when the joke's on you.
- Remember that many times God uses our troubles as tools to improve us.
- Understand that bisexual is not sex twice a month.
- Remember that the advantage of exercising every day is that you die healthier.
- Use your stomach as a lap tray unless it's smothered by your bust.
- Thank God for deciding that babies are a nice way to start people.

These deeply "spiritual" insights have been great sources of uplift for me when I'm having a gloomy day and tending to hold on to my troubles, regrets, and sorrows. Again, my faith in God's deliverance is what helps me to release them. So what does it mean to truly let go?

Letting Go

To let go doesn't mean to stop caring; it means I can't do it for someone else.

To let go is not to cut myself off; it's the realization that I can't control another.

To let go is not to enable but to allow learning from natural consequences.

To let go is to admit powerlessness, which means that the outcome is not in my hands.

To let go is not to try to change or blame another; I can change only myself.

To let go is not to care for but to care about.

To let go is not to fix but to be supportive.

To let go is not to judge but to allow another to be a human being.

To let go is not to be in the middle arranging all the outcomes but to allow others to affect their own outcomes.

To let go is not to be protective; it is to permit another to face reality.

To let go is not to deny but to accept.

To let go is not to nag, scold, or argue but to search out my own shortcomings and to correct them.

To let go is not to adjust everything to my desires but to take each day as it comes and to cherish the moment.

To let go is not to criticize and regulate anyone but to try to become what I dream I can be.

To let go is not to regret the past but to grow and live for the future.

To let go is to fear less and love more.

In order to truly relinquish control, we need to believe that God is able to take care of our struggles, situations, and sorrows. The same hands that formed the universe are big enough to handle life's challenges and disasters.

When we truly trust God, we'll get to the point where we're not afraid of anything. We have the assurance that regardless of what comes across our paths in the end, those of us who are on God's side will win. One of the most certain evidences of faith in God is when we can turn away from a tough situation in which we have done our best and are able to focus on other matters with a peaceful, calm mind. Then we can truly know that we have let go—and we're letting God control the situation.

What a comfort it is when we surrender the jangled fragments of our lives into the hands of God! Then we can experience the true joy that comes from knowing that although our lives and situations are out of our control, everything is going to be all right if we keep trusting the Lord.

And remember—even when you have a yard sale and no one shows up, your dog follows someone else home, or you can't afford the tuition for the school of hard knocks, hold onto your faith—and God will see you through!

Adapted in part from *Fresh Elastic for Stretched Out Moms,* Barbara Johnson (Old Tappan, New Jersey: Fleming H. Revell Co.), 162-72. Used by permission.

🖎 **Barbara Johnson** *is a popular author, speaker, and humorist with 15 books to her credit and more than 6 million copies in print. Her work centers on the healing lessons of love and laughter. She and her husband, Bill, live in La Habra, California.*

9 · Jo Edlin

FROM SHAME TO VICTORY

I had done a horrible thing—I had attempted to take my own life. God had forgiven me, but how could my life ever be normal again? Feelings of aloneness and hopelessness spun in my confused mind during my days as a patient in a psychiatric hospital.

As shocking as my attempted suicide was to those who knew me, to me it seemed the only logical option at the time. I could no longer cope with my manic-depressive illness. For many years I had functioned as a wife, mother, and nurse, but it seemed that the waves of depression were becoming harder and harder to hide. I had tried different medications and had quit my stressful job as a hospice nurse. But I didn't seek further help or share my desperation with anyone. I felt absolutely defeated.

So on June 11, 1999, I checked into a local hotel, double-locked the door, and moved the phone far away from the bed. At approximately 9:30 A.M. I poured my new three-month supply of medication into strawberry yogurt and quickly ate it. As soon as I swallowed the last of it, I started to panic. I sighed several times to relax myself and remembered what had brought me to this place: "Your family will be better off without you. You are useless in God's kingdom. Heaven will be such a relief." As I climbed under the cool, hotel-white sheets, I said a prayer: *God, if this is not Your will, then You'll have to intervene, because I don't know what else to do.*

I expected to wake up in heaven. But God intervened, and 26 hours later my family found me—miraculously alive. I felt very disappointed. I had not expected to face the guilt and shame that I experienced.

After a two-week hospitalization, I was sent to a psychiatric hospital for one week. My family was very supportive and visited me often. After my release, a wonderful therapist came to our home for several visits to help us work through our feelings. The new medicines were working, and I returned to my current job as an associate in sales. But I just couldn't seem to move forward past the shame.

I knew manic-depressive illness was a physical problem, and it was being treated with medication—just as diabetes or any other disease is managed. My problem was *shame*. I had done this and caused great heartache to the very ones I loved the most. I knew only my faith would lead me to healing.

When I was five years old I accepted God's forgiveness for my sins, and throughout my life He protected and provided for me. But as shame continued to plague me and I began having nightmares, I knew I needed a miracle. I realized that if someone tried to kill my daughter as I had tried to kill myself, only through God could I forgive that person.

During my counseling session on February 13, 2001, I told the Christian therapist whom the Lord had brought into my life that I needed God to cleanse me from my shame. Immediately, that small office became a sanctuary as she and I prayed together. The shame was gone, and in its place—peace!

My life was getting back to normal, and the memory of the suicide attempt was becoming blurred. But God had more healing in store—for me and for others. In September 2001, my pastor asked me to share my testimony. I knew it was what I needed to do. If my story could prevent one person from making the mistake I had made, it would be worth it. It was very difficult to relive those intense emotions as I read my journal, but my faith in God sustained me.

Since my testimony that September Sunday, my husband

and I have shared our story many times. The feedback has been very positive, especially from many people who have experienced the same or similar problems.

Of course, I would rather not have this long-term illness. And I'm so sorry my family had to go through this experience. But God has been faithful to me, and He has used my illness to minister to others. Since I have unmasked my life and allowed God to use me, I have found a new joy in increased faith.

My faith is in the God who was watching over me in that hotel room.

My faith is in the God who gives me the courage to share my story.

My faith is securely attached to the God who has designed a beautiful future for me.

And my faith is in the God who has healed me from my shame and given me victory.

 Jo Edlin *is a retired nurse. Her husband, Jim, is a university professor in the Kansas City area. They reside in Olathe, Kansas.*

10 ❧ Hephzi David

SPREADING THE FAITH

Even though I grew up very poor in Palayamkotai, India, and we had only very simple food to eat, I was very rich because we had a Christian home. My father took me to church every Sunday and taught me from the Bible. At 5 A.M. each morning we had family devotions and woke up our neighbors with our singing.

In 1956, when I was in the 10th grade, Billy Graham held a great crusade in our area. As he shared about the love of God, I began to evaluate myself. I had thought that I was a good Christian because of my heritage and church activities. But as the Lord spoke to me through Dr. Graham's message, I realized that I was a sinner and needed to be forgiven. With tears flowing down my face, I went forward and committed my life to the Lord. As I walked home that evening, I cried tears of joy, praising God and thanking Him for my new life in Jesus Christ. My parents' faith had truly become mine as well.

After completing high school and college, I taught school and then became the principal of a private high school. Then God changed the course of my life by calling me into full-time Christian service.

When I submitted my resignation, the authorities refused to accept it. They were pleased with my performance and the progress of the school, so they made it difficult for me to leave. They told me, "If you resign, you must pay one month's salary." There was no way I could come up with that amount. The only thing of value that I had was a gold chain. As I prayed, I told the Lord that I was very willing to sell my chain if that was necessary. Then He spoke to me from Ps. 57:2—"I will cry unto God most high; unto God that performeth all things for me" (KJV). I claimed that promise and prayed continuously for God's will to be done. When I submitted my resignation the second time, the school authorities said, "We don't want to stop you from serving your God." That was a miracle! My faith had been rewarded.

When I resigned my job, I had no idea what God wanted me to do. He gave me the faith to believe that He would provide for me and make His will clear. I began to look for open doors of ministry. One day I was asked to share my testimony at a youth rally before more than 2,000 people.

The Lord had impressed me to be very open and transparent about my early failures as a student. He told me that this would help a broken soul. I was trembling as I shared my story with that huge crowd. Afterward, a young schoolgirl ran to me with tears and said, "Akka [Sister], I have a bottle of rat poison in my hand. I had intended to commit suicide after this meeting because of my failing grades. Your testimony has given me hope. Now I want to live for Jesus." She threw the bottle of poison into the trash and went back to her room.

I applied to be a missionary to the islands, but they told me I was too young. My faith held steady, and I trusted God for His timing. Finally the Lord opened the doors for me to join India Youth for Christ. It was a joy to work among the young people, which I did for 21 years, leading many young girls and couples to the Lord.

God led Christopher David, a dedicated Christian young man, into my life. We were married in 1971 and had wonderful ministries among the young people in India Youth for Christ. The Lord has blessed us with three marvelous children.

Our faith has been tested many times through these years. We were transferred five times while we were with Youth for Christ. Every relocation required steps of faith. Our children faced many adjustments each time we moved.

On Christmas Day 1978 we were in a new city, and all five of

us were sick. There was no one to help us or to provide any food. Miraculously, God met our needs—He healed us and sent friends with food. He had always answered our prayers, and our faith held steady. Regardless of the obstacles, we learned to keep spreading the faith with determination.

During our years in Hyderabad, eight of us were living in one bedroom along with cats and rats. Our office was in that tiny home as well. One day when we returned from a staff conference, we found that a boy we had been helping had stolen everything of value and run away. We were discouraged and heartbroken. But the Lord remained faithful to us in the midst of this loss, as He had in sickness and in other disappointments.

When we were transferred to Calcutta, we could not find an affordable place to live. Both of us were teaching school and taking care of a church and our children. Although our circumstances were very challenging, it was rewarding to spread the good news of the gospel among the physically and spiritually hungry people of Calcutta. Once again, God was faithful to us.

While we were in Calcutta God opened the door for us to work with Robert Cunville, an associate evangelist with the Billy Graham Evangelistic Association, to coordinate the Festivals of Peace in India. This has been a special blessing to me, since I committed my life to the Lord under Billy Graham's ministry. We continue enjoying our work with this wonderful ministry.

Teaching has always been very rewarding to me. I recently completed my master of arts degree in Christian psychology and counseling, and that has opened more opportunities for me to share my faith. Once when I had the joy of leading a young girl to the Lord, her father became very angry. He tried to sue me in court. It was a very frightening time. We prayed fervently and held onto our faith in God. Once again, He delivered me.

Christopher and I rejoice today that many of the young men and women we led to the Lord and counseled and discipled over the years are now in the ministry and are spreading the gospel.

Hephzi David   41

All three of our children are serving the Lord with their time and talents. Our youngest son, Paul, resigned his lucrative computer job to enter full-time ministry.

I praise the Lord for His grace in honoring our faith. He has held us steady through many challenging situations. My heart is filled with joy as I reflect on the wonderful years that He has given to us. We are determined to continue the work—not just keeping the faith but spreading it as well.

*Hephzi David **is the executive secretary of the Robert Cunville Festivals for the Billy Graham Evangelistic Association. She is a Christian counselor and psychologist and speaks for many conferences. She and her husband, Christopher, live in Bangalore, India.***

Section 2

Either He will shield you from suffering

or He will give you unfailing strength

to bear it.

Be at peace, then.

—Francis de Sales

11 ✺ Gloria Gaither

NOW I KNOW THAT THIS IS NOT A SPRINT — BUT A MARATHON

When I was in elementary school in Burlington, Michigan, we had what were called "field days." The whole school was involved, and we could sign up ahead of time for the field event for which we felt most suited. There were the standing broad jump, the running broad jump, the high jump, the discus throw, the relay race, the 100-yard dash, and others.

I wasn't very athletic. I couldn't even throw a softball well enough to make the girls' summer team, so discus throwing was out of my league entirely, and only tall girls with long legs seemed to excel at the 100-yard dash. But I always tried the running broad jump and the high jump. For the broad jump, someone stood at the side of the sawdust pit to mark and then measure how far from the jumping line one landed. Stronger, more graceful kids always beat me out in that one. The high jump was performed by jumping over a cane pole resting on pegs in two parallel vertical posts. The slightest touch would dislodge the pole. The object was to get a running start and then hurl one's body over the pole. Each successful try was followed by the official's moving the pole up one more increment on the posts. The long, lean type was always superior to me in that event.

You can understand, then, why the metaphor of a race has not been the scriptural comparison to most inspire me. A wave of fifth grade nausea always seemed to swell in my stomach whenever I read Heb. 12 and felt Paul start in on me as a runner and the spiritual journey as a field day event.

But now that I'm older and wiser, I'm coming to believe that the race so often referred to in the Bible is not a 100-yard dash or a broad jump (running or standing) or a high jump or a discus throw. These verses aren't even about winning. The race, I'm discovering, is not a sprint—it's a marathon. And the object of this life event is to *finish!*

It doesn't matter whether I run, jog, or eventually manage to drag my pulsating, throbbing body over the finish line. The point is to finish, to get there without quitting. Whenever I think I can't go another inch, a support team is running alongside to catch me when my knees buckle. Fans in the bleachers all along the well-planned and carefully chosen course have long since found this race possible by finishing it themselves. At every bend in the track, there they are, cheering and encouraging me at the top of their lungs: "Yes, you can! You can make it!" In the Body of Christ that's what friends are for.

And I'm finally coming to know that endurance is what the Coach is after. He's not interested in spurts of flashy athletic prowess. He isn't impressed by sleek bodies, rippling muscles, or perfect physiques. It's determination that He adores. It's the earnest pursuit of the goal that makes Him proud. It's the beauty of the gift of commitment to the experience itself—staying the course, keeping the faith, and enjoying the journey.

The trophy is engraved not with "First Place Winner," not with "Most Valuable Player"—but with "Faithful unto the End." Even I can sign up with confidence for that. I may not be good, but I can be stubbornly persistent to the end.

From *Confessions of Four Friends Through Thick and Thin,* Gloria Gaither (Grand Rapids, Michigan: Zondervan Publishing House, 2001). Used by permission.

Gloria Gaither *has written more than 400 songs and numerous major musicals. She is an author and speaker as well as scriptwriter for the Homecoming Video Series. She recorded for 20 years with the Bill Gaither Trio. Gloria and her husband, Bill, live in Alexandria, Indiana.*

12 ❧ Kerrie Grace

FAITH, FEAR, AND FINANCES

I remember clearly a lecture at Hillsong Conference 2000 by Pastor Al Bernard of New York. "Fear is the opposite of faith," he said. Those words pierced my spirit. Through the early years of our ministry, I was full of fear. Fear for our finances was a major one.

I thought back to 1997 when my husband, Steve, organized an eight-week evangelistic tour of Australia designed to take the gospel to isolated outback regions of central and western Australia. We put together a small team of four crew members and four families, including our own.

As we started discussing the idea of the tour, we were amazed at how quickly it all came together. The towns in the Northern Territory were eager to have us, and God started providing sponsorship in very practical ways. One family's fuel was sponsored, and a vehicle was supplied to another family. For our family of five, the Lord supplied a caravan with a shower and a toilet, which was an answer to my prayers and confirmation that God really does hear the prayers of a mother.

God had impressed upon us the urgency for evangelism, so we took a step of faith and began presenting free concerts so the gospel would be accessible to all. Many of the towns we planned to visit were quite remote and isolated, and most artists and evangelists did not tour them. Even though we knew the concerts to be held in many of these places would not provide the finances to cover our costs, we believed the gospel was to go to them too, and we trusted God to provide. We had always had good concerts in Perth, so we added that city to our tour, trusting the income from those concerts would help finance concerts in the more remote areas up north.

The first part of the tour was amazing. As we presented our concerts, Steve preached, and people came to know Jesus. Some of the areas were suffering through a drought, so Steve prayed for rain. Sure enough, those prayers were answered. Our spirits were high, and the Lord was providing the finances to pay our bills as well.

To our dismay, when we reached Perth, the concerts there did not go so well. Even with all the preparation, advertising, publicity, and promotions, attendance was down. Our team had been on the road for five straight weeks, and fatigue was setting in. Morale began to run low.

After leaving Perth, we gave two more concerts, one in Geraldton and one in Carnarvon. Neither concert was well attended. Afterward we walked away with barely enough profit to get us through the next few days of travel and accommodations. I remember the fear that began to grip me as I balanced the books.

We had just paid off the debt we incurred when we recorded our first album. I knew that if we went back into debt it would delay our dream of owning our first home. We prayed, "Lord, what do You want us to do? Our eyes are on You, and we want to be good stewards."

During a three-day break in our schedule on the coast of western Australia that we had planned to use for rest and relaxation, Steve and I found ourselves seriously contemplating calling it a day. If we canceled the remainder of the tour and drove the 5,000 kilometers home, we would just about break even financially. It seemed to be the sensible thing to do. The crew was worn out, and spirits were low. We had had the funds to pay our expenses so far. But if we kept going, the odds were that we would end up with a large debt at the end of the tour.

During that three-day break in our schedule, the Lord clearly reminded us that we had never quit before. If we had truly heard

from God to embark on this adventure in the first place, then we needed to stand on His Word and allow Him to use us—no matter what the outcome. We had promised people that we were coming, and we chose to honor our word.

The concerts we held over the next four weeks went well—at Broome, Derby, and Port Hedland. The people were so appreciative, and it was a privilege to serve these churches and people who are so far away from the major cities and towns. Upon arrival in Darwin, Steve and I checked the finances and resigned ourselves to the fact that we would probably arrive home owing about $18,000. There was always the option of recouping our costs by selling the block of land that God had recently provided us. Each day we prayed and trusted God to provide for our needs.

The Darwin concert, the last on our tour, was fantastic. It was such an encouragement to our team to end with such a great, appreciative crowd. Steve preached well, and people came to know Jesus. We were all ready to go home, satisfied that we had completed the adventure to which God had called us.

Back at home, we received many encouraging letters and E-mails. People shared their testimonies and thanked us for coming so far to minister to them and asked us to return someday. It always humbles me to read some of the mail and to know that God is touching people's lives through our ministry.

Going over the final figures for the tour, we realized that we were out of pocket exactly $20,000. Steve was away on another booking, and I phoned him to inform him so that he could pray. We prayed together over the phone and totally gave the situation to Jesus.

The very next day as I was working in the office, a lady called to share with me that she had attended our concert in Darwin and was greatly blessed. She mentioned that she had been praying and knew that we did not have enough money to cover the tour expenses. She asked me what the shortfall was. I was surprised and a bit hesitant to discuss this with someone I didn't know. I asked her if I could E-mail her a breakdown of the costs, as this would allow me a bit of time to think and pray about whether I should share this or not.

After I hung up, I asked Colleen, the financial administrator for Steve Grace Ministries, what she thought I should do, and she replied simply, "You should tell the truth." So I E-mailed the breakdown of our expenses, clearly showing what we still owed. The next day this lady phoned back and said that she would like to send a check for the entire $20,000 as a gift to our ministry.

I couldn't believe it! Could this be true? I decided not to say anything to Steve or anyone else until I saw the check. Seven days later I was collecting the mail, and there it was—a check for $20,000 from an anonymous donor who had been at the Darwin concert.

I sat in the car and cried. How awesome God is! I thought about how close we came to turning around, coming home without completing the tour. I realized that not only would that have hindered God's plans for ministering to the people of those remote towns, but we would have missed the miracle of His provision. God waited until the very last concert and moment to answer our prayers and provide our needs to the exact cent.

As stated by Al Bernard, "Fear is the opposite of faith. Fear is to the negative what faith is to the positive."

🌾 **Kerrie Grace** *works with her husband, Steve, in their international music ministry. They live with their three sons in Queensland, Australia.*

13 ❧ Joyce Williams

THE OTHER SIDE OF THE PROMISE

The shrill ringing of the telephone jerked me awake. I glanced at the illuminated clock by the bed as I clumsily groped for the phone. 11 P.M.

"Hello?"

Christy's soft voice penetrated my sleepy fog. Our granddaughter had been going through a very difficult time and was in another stage of heartbreak. I listened carefully.

Knowing what a morning person I am and that I'm notorious for fading out early in the evening, Christy first apologized for waking me. She didn't even realize that her grandpa was out of town and that I was home alone.

She said, "I've been reading Job, and I have a question about a certain passage. Could you tell me what it means?" Then she began to read Job 11:14-19. I was wide awake now, and I began to quote those precious and familiar words along with her there in the dark. Could I ever begin to tell her about the wonderful promise in those words!

I exclaimed, "Christy! Exactly 10 years ago God gave that very same passage to me—just when I needed it most! This is awesome. Now He's given it to you! Let me tell you from the other side of the promise what it's meant in my life."

So I began my story. On a hot summer day in 1990, I was driving home to Roanoke, Virginia, from a meeting in Richmond. My marriage of more than 26 years had ended, and my life was torn apart with grief, rejection, and uncertainty. As I drove along, it also occurred to me that for the first time in my life I was going to have to spend the night by myself. For whatever reason, I was terrified to think of being alone in our big house. Fear clutched my heart as I cried out to the Lord, *I can't do this! Would You please help me?* I believe those are some of God's favorite words to hear from us!

I had been listening to a Christian radio station as I approached Lynchburg, Virginia. When a particular song ended, the announcer said, "I have a scripture for someone who really needs it." And he began to read from Job 11:

> If you put away the sin that is in your hand and allow no evil to dwell in your tent, then you will lift up your face without shame; you will stand firm and without fear. You will surely forget your trouble, recalling it only as waters gone by. Life will be brighter than noonday, and darkness will become like morning. You will be secure, because there is hope; you will look about you and take your rest in safety. You will lie down, with no one to make you afraid *(Job 11:14-19)*.

As I heard the beautiful promises, I felt the paralyzing fear leave my body. I could almost visualize the anxieties disappearing through the roof of my car. Waves of healing and hope flooded through my soul, and tears of joy streamed down my face as I pulled over to the side of the road. In that metal cathedral, I felt God's love and kindness wrap around me as never before. And it was a complete healing. As I climbed into bed that night, all fear was gone. I spent that night, and many other nights since, alone with absolutely no fear.

I reminded Christy that a few months later, the Lord reinstated His call on my life to full-time ministry. I was amazed. In the midst of my rejection, God said He wanted me! Through an incredible series of events, He led me to Clearwater, Florida, to be on staff at a church there.

A year and a half after I went to Clearwater, Brian Arner, a wonderful, talented singer and member of the church, introduced me to Christy's grandpa, who was pastoring a church in Wichita, Kansas. His dear wife of many years had died very suddenly more than a year prior to that time. After a long-distance courtship and

whirlwind romance, we were married in September 1992, and I moved to Wichita. Immediately I inherited a wonderful extended family, including Christy and 12 other grandchildren. (I've told Gene I would have married him just for those grandkids!)

God has continued to open incredible doors of blessing and opportunity for me in speaking, writing, and other ministries. In January 1998 Gene resigned after 47 years of pastoring, and we began Shepherds' Fold Ministries for ministerial families. Also, we both have worked on special assignments with the Billy Graham Evangelistic Association as well as many, many other wonderful opportunities.

I said, "Christy, Honey, you have no idea what God has planned for your life. You're just on the threshold. All I can say is that when God gave Job 11 to me a decade ago, I would not have dared to ask Him for all that He has done for me. Surely I have forgotten my troubles. I can barely remember them, and my life is brighter than dawn. Our security comes in the hope of Jesus."

And I reminded her of the deep valley through which Job was walking when God gave that promise to him so long ago. We quickly agreed that none of our troubles compared with Job's. "Yet," I reminded her, "Job has a chapter 42. Verse 12 reads, 'The LORD blessed the latter part of Job's life more than the first.'"

With absolute confidence, I said, "You can make it. God's promises are still good today. It doesn't matter where you've been or where you are. It's where you go from here that's important. Just stay focused on the Lord, and He'll get you through. The sun will shine for you once again. I can tell you for sure—because I've been there. The promise given to Job still works today. Read the end of the book!"

Then I prayed with Christy, said good night, and hung up the phone. Although Gene was away from home, I was neither alone nor afraid. As I laid there in the dark basking in the light of the Son, I drifted off to sleep thanking Him for chapter 42!

14 ❧ Alicia Griffin

GOD SINGS A LOVE SONG

I grew up with seven siblings and four adopted cousins. My life in the Mexican town of Hacienda El Carmen, Tamaulipas, was many things, but it was never boring.

My mother became a Christian when I was eight years old, and she was the most influential person in my life. Her unwavering faith, persistence, and sacrifice formed me into the person I am today.

I have many fond memories of my childhood, but that memory is stained by my father's violence toward my mother when he was drunk. All of us were affected by his erratic behavior, and we were scarred emotionally and spiritually by his instability. As a result of the chronic stress and unresolved emotional pain, I grew to feel unlovable and undeserving of happiness and love and respect. At times I was overwhelmed by depression, feelings of failure, and even thoughts of suicide.

We were very involved in our church, and our religious activities delighted our mother. Finally I came to realize that I was trying to satisfy God and my mother by doing good things. I had to acknowledge that those good things were for the most part "dead works." I continued to attend church, but I didn't have the joy of the Lord in my life, and my faith was very weak.

The Lord began to show me the dark areas of my life and gave me a spirit of repentance. Although I was in a spiritual and emotional desert, God spoke tenderly to me so that He could restore what the enemy had taken from me through hurt, blame, bitterness, and unforgiveness.

In that dry and thirsty desert I finally began to understand that nothing perpetuates the impact of hurts more than rehashing them, and I discovered that bemoaning our fate doesn't help heal our past. For the first time I truly realized that God, in His inexhaustible wonder, grace, and unconditional love, will fill our hearts if we will let Him. When I began seeking His face with my whole heart and abandoned myself into His care, He created a hunger within me to know Him and to seek Him for who He is rather than for what I would receive by serving Him.

As I read Zeph. 3:17 one day, I could almost hear Him singing a song of love over me. I totally surrendered to the Lord, and He began to work in my life in marvelous ways. The faith that I discovered was my own, not just an extension of my mother's.

The love of my Heavenly Father enabled me to begin to see my earthly father in a different light. My dad was tall, handsome, very charismatic, and he praised us for our accomplishments. He was a great storyteller and very creative. We were all thankful when he quit drinking in the later years of his life.

Finally, I went to my dad to ask him to forgive me for my thoughts about him in the past. I could tell that he had been totally unaware of the ways in which his actions and excuses had affected all our lives. He took my hands and said, "I'm sorry. Will you forgive me?" Both of us cried. I felt a wonderful sense of release as God's healing flowed over me and swept away years of bitterness.

Shortly after I graduated from college, I was married. In the next few years we had three children. Our marriage was not what I expected it would be, and I felt discouraged. However, we managed to hold our marriage together, although our relationship was very unhealthy.

During that time the Lord helped me to see my husband in a new way. God has blessed our lives, and our children and grandchildren are great blessings to us. The Lord has given me a successful dental practice.

God has opened many doors of opportunity for me to share

my testimony and faith in Him. Of course, I have a captive audience when a patient is seated in my dental chair! I love telling people that faith in God is the only answer to life's questions and problems. We must never be satisfied with less than God's best.

I thank my mom for her heritage of prayers and faith. Her encouragement to live the abundant life still motivates me today to be satisfied with nothing less than God's best plan. She always told us never to give up. Her faithfulness and our prayers were answered when my dad accepted the Lord before he died.

I've found that when we're in a storm and are being tossed by stress and pain and grief, we must courageously cling to God's promises. With faith we can come to understand that broken dreams are not the end of dreaming, and disappointment is not the end of hope. Because of God, today's failures can point us to tomorrow's victories.

On days when the hours are long and I'm worried, I pause to listen to my Heavenly Father. That's when, once again, He sings a love song over me.

Alicia Griffin is a dentist who has lived in the United States for more than 32 years. She is involved in the Nashville Hispanic Chamber of Commerce and hosts the radio program "Your Health and Your Soul." Alicia and her husband, John, live in Nashville.

15 ❧ Jan Harvey

THE CONSTANT CALL OF FAITH

It seemed like a normal, relaxing summer day at the beach. I had a good book, a new beach chair, and five hours to sit in the sand and take in the smells and sounds of the surf. Little did I know a few hours spent in that chair would result in a herniated lumbar disk. Since when did relaxing on the beach carry such heavy consequences?

Several days and one MRI (magnetic resonance imaging) later, the diagnosis came from my orthopedic surgeon: "You've *really* done it this time. Cancel your schedule for the next three weeks!" I was to undergo removal of my lumbar disk the very next day. It was performed without much fanfare, and, as I was told, it went rather well.

The real problem came later that week when I developed severe pain in my left leg. It was a deep vein thrombosis—a blood clot to you and me—that had broken loose after my doctor squeezed my sore calf muscle. The clot broke into several pieces, which we realized was a good thing, but the pieces moved into my lungs. The term "pulmonary embolism" means a lot more to me now than it used to. I ended up back in the hospital.

That night at the hospital there was great concern that a "mother clot" would dislodge and travel to my heart or my brain, causing a stroke. Meanwhile, the alien small clots had created pockets of fluid between my lungs and chest wall. The doctor promised to remove these in a "less than painless" procedure the next morning.

Throughout the night I thought about my life and tried to face the real possibility that by morning my life might be over. I was so uneasy and afraid. I couldn't feel God with me. I struggled to pray but felt spiritually alone. Why wasn't He giving me the peace I had always felt in crisis? Why at such a crucial time did He seem to abandon me? It was a long, anxious night. My husband, Don, and I said all the things you need to say to one another. And we waited.

Timing is the best part of any miracle. Morning came, and Don went home to get some fresh clothes. I was alone reading my Bible. My new "nurse of the day" came in and commented, "I see you're reading the best book in the world."

After her routine exam, she asked, "Do you mind if I pray with you?" Surprised, I readily agreed, and she prayed. I thanked her, and she continued with her duties in the room.

After a few minutes of chatting, she paused. Then she said, "God's telling me something. I'm not sure what, but I don't want to miss it. Could we pray again?" I agreed, and this time the prayer was quite different—a "storming heaven" kind of prayer. I've never experienced a prayer like that.

After a few moments she said, "God has something to say to you. Can you receive it?" I was ready to receive anything I could get from God in any way He chose to reveal it. So she began, speaking in first person: *Don't be afraid. You have allowed your fear to make this solely a natural event. It is a spiritual one as well, and I am in control. Your healing has begun. You have asked Me recently how you can serve Me better—this will be a part of that service. I will bring people into your life who will need to hear this. Be bold. I am with you.*

I was astounded and laid there trying to process what I had just heard. She quoted a scripture and turned to leave. Then she paused and said, "Oh, and that procedure you're so worried about—you're not going to need it."

I began to pray. And as I did, the supernatural peace that comes only from the Father flooded my heart. I did a 180-degree emotional turn. The fear was gone. At that point it didn't matter whether or not I lived. The struggle of whether or not God was with me was over, and that was all that mattered.

Later that morning my daughter, Paige, came in with a wonderful book, *The Esther Effect*. She read to me for a while. The author spoke of the "Esthers" in our lives who dare to speak or perform God's will in spite of the consequences. Mordecai told Esther as she chose to go before the king for her people, "Who knows whether you have come to this kingdom for such a time as this?" (Esther 4:14, NKJV). I realized my nurse was my Esther. She chose to obey God in spite of her professional role and her potential embarrassment. In doing so, she gave me more than any medicine could.

What she gave was God's promise to me—assurance that He had not left me alone with my fear in that hospital room. Isn't God tender in our crises? When He doesn't seem to speak directly through Scripture or prayer, or even the nurse of the day, I am assured that He is no less present in my quiet times than He was in my darkest hour. I don't understand why God chooses to reveal himself at some times and not others. But I have truly learned that faith is a constant call—believing fervently, trusting quietly, and resting in His loving covenant. He's actively at work even when we can't see His hand!

By the way, I didn't have to have that procedure to drain my lungs.

"Now I know that the LORD saves His anointed; He will answer him from His holy heaven with the saving strength of His right hand. Some trust in chariots, and some in horses; but we will remember the name of the LORD our God" (Ps. 20:6-7, NKJV).

🌾 **Jan Harvey** *is a marriage and family therapist in Nashville and serves as a career counselor at Trevecca Nazarene University. She and husband, Don, also a marriage and family therapist, conduct marriage weekends, speak at professional conferences, and serve as therapy fellows at Marble Retreat (for clergy couples) in Colorado.*

16 Angie Hillman

FALLING IN LOVE WITH JESUS

I had been in the midst of considerable brokenness for 18 months when the vice president of marketing came into my office to discuss my request for some time off. After talking for more than an hour, she started out the door. In desperation, I reached across my desk and said, "I feel better now that we've talked, but I feel as if I have a huge hole in my heart, and nothing will fill it."

She turned and spoke six words that changed my life forever: "You need God in your life."

The next thing I knew, I was praying the sinner's prayer, although I didn't have a clue about what that meant. When I was finished, I thought, *Whew! Now I know I'm going to heaven, and I can get on with the rest of my life!* Little did I know that God had other plans.

I call the next eight months purgatory. I hadn't grown up in church and didn't feel comfortable going to one. Also, I got physically ill before I was supposed to meet my friends for a night out on the town.

Finally I went to church. It was there that I learned that Christianity is more than a ticket to heaven. I began reading the Bible for the first time and discovered in Matt. 7 that you could ask and receive. So I prayed and asked God to give me a husband or *someone to fill the gap*. That last phrase is an important one, because I had always had boyfriends who had lavished me with generous gifts—from trips around the country to furnishings for my apartment to helping me buy a car. I wasn't accustomed to being on my own. That's why I prayed for a husband or *someone to fill the gap*.

One verse in my Bible study was "Be still, and know that I am

God" (Ps. 46:10). That was the first time I felt God speak to me through His Word. From then on, I spent almost every waking moment reading my Bible and getting to know God.

Two years later, the Lord moved me to a beautiful beach town. He had transformed my life to such an extent that I hardly recognized myself. One night I walked along the beach and told the Lord that I would love to share my new life with someone. Once again, I asked Him for a husband.

A few days later I got a note from a friend. At the bottom of it was written "Psalm 27:14." I ran to my Bible to find out what it said, sensing that this was an answer to my request for a husband. Much to my dismay, it was. It read, "Wait for the LORD; be strong and take heart and wait for the LORD." I was so disappointed. When I mentioned my disappointment to a friend at work, his response floored me. He said, "You're right where my wife was before she met me. She realized she needed to fall in love with the Lord before she could love someone else." I pondered that strange comment for days and finally came to the conclusion that I read the Word and prayed out of a sense of obligation—not love. I realized that my heart was not right. That night I asked the Lord to teach me how to fall in love with Him. I even giggled when I prayed it, because I had known Him as Provider, but I wasn't sure if He could answer a request that was so personal. I was in for the shock of my life.

A few days later, a friend called to invite me to attend a women's retreat after someone had dropped out at the last minute. She said they asked God to pick the person He wanted to come. My name was chosen out of a hat. All I knew about the retreat was that it was called "Tres Días" and that it meant "three days" with the Lord.

I was so excited when I learned I had been selected to attend. When I told my friend what my prayer had been, there was dead silence on the other end of the phone. In shock, she said "I don't know if I should tell you this, but each weekend is based on

Angie Hillman

a scripture verse, and this one is based on Hos. 2:16, 19-20. It says, "'In that day,' declares the LORD, "you will call me 'my husband'; you will no longer call me 'my master.' . . . I will betroth you to me forever; I will betroth you in righteousness and justice, in love and compassion. I will betroth you in faithfulness, and you will acknowledge the LORD."'"

I stood there and wept. As my roommate watched the whole scene unfold, she asked what was happening. All I could say was, "Man, He is flippin' me out!" The flame of my fledgling faith was ignited.

That weekend I was courted by the Lord as no one else had ever done, and I had been wooed by the best of them. All my favorite things were there, and the whole weekend was a wedding. At the end of the three days I went to the altar and promised that I would never ask for a husband again, and I told Him that I would let Him be my husband. That's when the real adventure began, and my faith grew.

The Lord made himself known to me in hundreds of ways. I'll share with you a couple of my favorite stories.

One night I was getting ready for bed and a sample of perfume fell off my makeup tray. I held it up and thought, *Lord, it's been so long since I've had perfume, because it was the men in my life who used to buy it for me.* I immediately caught myself and confessed that I would rather have Him than a bottle of perfume. Life with Him had become so much sweeter than any relationship I had experienced with a man. The very next night I went to a Christmas party where door prizes were being given away. They held up a huge fragrance basket from a major department store and called my name. As I went to get my perfume I thought, *My Husband gave this perfume to me!*

Fourteen months later, I was attending a church with a congregation of around 75. As the pastor announced the upcoming Valentine's dinner, I thought, *I'm definitely not going to that!* I was one of only four singles in the entire church. Then the

Lord gently spoke to my heart and said, *I want you to go*. So I threw my name into the offering plate.

A few days later as I was getting ready to go to the dinner, a coworker asked me why I didn't have a valentine. (People get concerned if you're over 30 and unmarried!) I explained to him that the Lord was my Valentine. Although he was impressed with what the Lord had done in my life, his response to me was, "That's great. But you still need flesh and blood."

I replied, "No, I really don't." But when I thought about that, I realized that there was one thing I missed about not having a boyfriend, and that was getting a massage. I worked out and was constantly sore across my shoulders. Nearly every day I would say out loud, *Lord, if You could just give me a massage, I would never need a man*. My coworkers thought I was crazy. What I didn't realize was that God was about to take my faith to a new level.

When I arrived at my church for the Valentine's dinner, they were giving away door prizes. They held up this really pretty necklace, and I thought, *Lord, I would love that*. But I didn't win it. Then I thought, *Lord, You must have something else for me*, because I knew He wouldn't take me to a Valentine's dinner and not give me a present. The next prize was a one-hour massage—and I won it! My boss, who had heard me say that crazy thing to the Lord almost every day, sat across from me in amazement and said, "I don't know how you do that."

I replied, "I *don't*—but He *does*."

In the beginning, when the Lord told me to be still and get to know Him, if I had known that it would be seven years before I dated again, I think I would have been less enthusiastic. Yet when the Lord told me that He was about to bring a husband into my life and it would be the best thing that ever happened to me besides Him, I screamed. The thought of someone coming between us was terrifying to me. He had done such an incredible work in my heart that I didn't want a husband anymore. I just wanted Him. That was enough miracle for me.

Angie Hillman

A month later I met the man who would become my husband, and we married nine months later. I must say, though, that even though I am happily married to a wonderful man, Jesus remains the greatest romance of my life. He has taken me, a person who was not seeking Him, and transformed my life in a way that is best described in 1 Pet. 1:8—"Though you have not seen him, you love him; and even though you do not see him now, you believe in him and are filled with an inexpressible and glorious joy."

God has been more than faithful to me as my faith has grown over these years. I'm so glad He courted me and loves me. He is an awesome husband! And I'm grateful that He gave me the faith to truly fall in love with Him!

🌿 **Angie Hillmann** *and her husband, Os, were married in 1998. Today they share a great ministry and testimony of their faith in God. They reside in Cumming, Georgia.*

17 ❦ Dinah Huff

A JOURNEY OF FAITH

I didn't know what to expect as we rushed up to the ticket counter. My husband, Fred, and I, along with our four-year-old son, Shane, were in Dallas, on the third leg of our journey to our first missionary assignment in Auckland, New Zealand. Our clear instructions from the World Mission Department were to pay all our bills before leaving the country. The Lord made provision to take care of everything except $800. Now here we were, on our way! From Dallas we would fly to Honolulu and then to Auckland. That last $800 was weighing heavily, but I was reminded of the words of 2 Cor. 5:7—"We walk by faith, not by sight" (KJV). Did that promise also include flying by faith?

As we arrived at our gate, the ticket agent informed us that our flight was sold out. Then he asked, "Would you consider staying overnight in Dallas? We'd be glad to provide motel and food vouchers for you along with cash." Since we had no deadline, we promptly replied, "Yes, of course." Imagine our amazement when he handed us the vouchers along with $1,000 cash. God had paid off our remaining debt with $200 left over! We vowed that the extra $200 would be our first deposit into a savings account when we settled in New Zealand.

The next morning when we returned to the airport, there was a long line at the ticket counter. Fred got in line, and the lady in front of him told him that this flight was also overbooked. Fred ran to the counter and told the agent we would be glad to volunteer our seats. Before we knew it, we were spending a second night in a hotel with free meals and another $1,000. Now our "bonus" amount had climbed to $1,200. I told Fred, "I have an idea—let's call our district superintendent in New Zealand and see if we could stay here 30 more days. Just think of the money we could make!"

On the third day, we arrived at the airport in a terrible storm. Tornadoes had been sighted in the area. To be very honest, we were hoping this flight would be overbooked as well. But this was our day to fly. After several delays, our plane took off. In just a few minutes we encountered ferocious winds, and the plane began to bounce around like a yo-yo. I've never been so frightened. Shane laughed and enjoyed it as though he were taking a roller coaster ride.

It was obvious to all of us onboard that our plane had sustained some damage. Some of the other passengers knew that we were young missionaries headed to our first assignment. One of them said, "Please pray, Preacher." And we did.

Finally the pilot was able to land in Houston. We sat on the plane for more than six hours while the damages were repaired. It seemed we would never get out of Texas!

As we waited, I reflected on the years that brought us to that point. Fred and I met at a Christian college. We each had been called to full-time Christian ministry and soon fell in love.

As Fred neared graduation, he sought God's will for his first assignment. Gene Williams, a pastor in Wichita, Kansas, called him to interview for the position of youth pastor. The interview went well, but Pastor Williams said, "We'd love to have you, but I need a married youth pastor." Fred responded with a gleam in his eye, "I think I can arrange that!" A few weeks later we were married and headed to the Land of Oz.

We had great years in Wichita. From there we accepted an assignment in Nashville. After several years the Lord began to nudge Fred toward a mission assignment overseas. Initially I wasn't very excited about that. It was one thing to move around the country, but an entirely different challenge to go to a new culture in a new country and leave behind our friends and families. My faith was tested as we prayed for God's will.

We applied and were accepted and appointed to New Zealand. I lived in the promise of Prov. 3:5-6: "Trust in the LORD with all your heart and lean not on your own understanding; in all your ways acknowledge him, and he will make your paths straight."

Sitting on that battered plane, I found my heart swelling with joy. The Lord had done just that! As Fred and I talked, we were more eager than ever to see what God had in store for us. We were leaving the country with our debts paid in full, and we even had a little nest egg now.

Pastoring in New Zealand was exciting for us, and our little congregation grew. The cement had been poured and the steel beams set for a new building before we arrived, and it was obvious the project needed to be completed. Fred went to several banks seeking a loan but was turned down each time. We prayed fervently. One day when Fred was praying, the Lord asked him, *What about the money I provided at the airport in Dallas?* Most of the money was drawing interest in a savings account. Immediately Fred replied, *Yes, Lord. I hear You.*

God gave Fred a challenging message for the following Sunday. At the close of his sermon, it was a joy to place a check from the savings account into the offering plate. After all, it was God's money! What a beautiful testimony of faith to see the significant amount of money that came in for the building fund. Those contributions along with funds from our general church enabled us to complete our building debt-free.

Today, looking back at the 31 years we have invested in ministry, it has been a joy to serve the Lord in a number of world areas. God has taught us many lessons in our faith journey, and He has never failed to provide everything we need. He's not usually been early, but He's certainly never been late. And the dividends on our investments are out of this world.

🌿 **Dinah Huff** *serves alongside her husband, Fred, who is regional director of the Africa Region for the Church of the Nazarene. Dinah is a speaker, mother, and grandmother.*

18 ❧ Dustee Hullinger

GIFTED HANDS

In 1969 I landed my dream job as a flight attendant with Trans World Airlines. For the next several years I was based in several locations in the United States. In 1975 I sensed the Lord was calling me to move from Los Angeles to New York City.

I had become a Christian when I was 13, and as a teenager I actively sought God's leading. When I sensed God beckoning me to a city in which I really had no previous desire to live, I reasoned that since New York is a hub for international travel, it would provide a way for me to accomplish my desire to travel around the world. I loved my job, and it was my gateway to different cultures, history, and art, and it provided the excitement I sought just about every day.

As a child I had felt God's call to missionary work, so traveling seemed a natural outgrowth of that call. As I struggled with God's call to New York, I finally understood that He was calling me to the concrete caverns of New York City rather than the jungles of Africa. He gave me the faith to step out on His promises, and I moved halfway across the country, anxious to find what He had in store for me.

During my travels with TWA, I crossed paths with flight attendants who belonged to a fellowship of Christian airline personnel. About 15 of them attended The Lamb's Church in Times Square, and they invited me to attend. The Lamb's Church overflowed with young, energetic Christians. The focus of the ministry was on the arts and evangelism. Pastor Paul Moore was a charismatic motivator, and I remember hearing him say, "Dream the dream, catch the vision, and God will open the door and give you the desires of your heart." My faith continued to grow.

The Lamb's was like no other church I had attended. Among its ministries was a Christian supper club, coffeehouses, concerts, as well as evangelism in parks, bars, and subways. The innovative thinking drew me like a magnet, and I realized I had found my place of worship. I surrendered my *entire* life to the Lord, and He changed me.

I confess that another big plus was that the Lamb's was filled with eligible Christian bachelors. Ultimately, that's where I met Jim Hullinger, my soul mate and husband of more than 26 years. Both of us remain very active members of the Lamb's.

Inspired by the Lamb's vision for inner-city ministry of working with the homeless, impoverished, and needy, I felt God's anointing to share the Good News with those who were hurting. I also felt called to motivate others into service, and I began collecting clothing from television stations, corporations, the airlines, and toiletries from hotels. As I traveled as a flight attendant, I talked about the Lamb's ministries to everyone who listened.

During my career I suffered several injuries that culminated in pain in my back, neck, spine, right arm, and right leg. The consensus of my doctors was that I must leave my job. Due to deteriorating disks, the consequences of continuing to work could be very serious.

During the next six months following my diagnosis, I was on disability and in great physical pain. I began a downward spiral physically and emotionally that left me questioning whether I would ever again enjoy a normal life and service to the Lord. Once again, God rewarded my faith.

At this time I attended a Make a Difference in Your World conference. As I listened to the speakers, God clearly impressed upon me that I was to work with the homeless and needy. In my spirit I answered, *Right. What could I possibly have in common with the homeless and the needy? I've been serving VIPs for 20 years. What could I offer someone who's homeless?*

It wasn't long before I was working in the Lamb's medical and foot clinic, where we soaked the feet of homeless men and told them of God's love. I found myself forming meaningful relationships with some of the street people of midtown New York. The Lord guided me into a deeper walk with Him through serving the needy. I began organizing fund-raisers and outreach dinners. I solicited volunteer dentists, doctors, podiatrists, and psychologists to help serve the indigent who frequented our homeless clinic. God continued to increase my faith as I served Him. The things that break His heart broke mine.

I heard that our church was starting a "peanut butter and jelly club" at a homeless family shelter in Harlem. I knew I could make sandwiches and tell children about Jesus. What I didn't know was that this would be the beginning of my real missionary work in New York City. When I asked the Lamb's director if I could teach an art and design class to young mothers while others ministered to their children, she agreed. I taught an eight-week art curriculum on art therapy and evangelism in the inner city.

That hands-on experience was life-changing. Broken, battered, and traumatized people opened up emotionally and formed a community. Wounded women began to feel like living again. I saw men and women develop self-esteem and awareness of their own value as they began to give back to society. Our students invited others to the classes, and leaders emerged as they began to sense their own empowerment. God introduced peace and tranquillity into the lives of people who had suffered severe trauma.

We distributed Bibles and began offering weekly inspirational devotions relating to the artwork. This created an opportunity to invite the students to church.

I was so moved by what the Lord did in those eight weeks that I sought funding to continue and was able to develop four more programs during the next two years. Several art classes were begun that included singing and drama lessons, and those

programs helped connect homeless and needy men to the church. Everyone was treated like a VIP, and friendships developed quickly.

Jim and I were blessed to develop Pathway to Wholeness, a program that integrated men into the church, created jobs, and focused on discipleship. This program allowed men to become self-sufficient and reenter mainstream living.

By 1996 a total of 15 programs throughout New York City had begun. That ministry, known as Gifted Hands, has now grown to 30 programs. Countless lives have been touched during these 10 years.

Gifted Hands offers an array of workshops taught by volunteer artists. We teach jewelry making, book making, sculpture, painting, tooled metal, mask making, cooking, decoupage, poetry, holiday crafts, pen-and-ink drawing, painted stained-glass, and woodworking classes.

The ministry operates with no paid staff and depends on financial donations and gifts-in-kind. The most recent gift to Gifted Hands was an unexpected donation of beautiful Austrian crystals and components. As a result, we have begun a jewelry making program through which our students learn design concepts and buying-and-selling principles.

I'm so humbled that God used me—a disabled flight attendant—to help make a difference in the inner city. But I'm reminded every day that through faith and reliance on God all things are possible.

I've watched a small grain of faith swell and develop into belief and hope for those who once were hopeless. Hands that were once empty are now filled with purpose and accomplishment and have become Gifted Hands.

🌿 **Dustee Hullinger** *founded and directs Gifted Hands, ministering through art and evangelism in more than 30 locations. She has worked in compassionate ministries at The Lamb's Church for more than 28 years. She and her husband, Jim, reside in Manhattan, New York.*

19 ✺ Lovincer Menya

A FULL HOUSE

My wedding day was filled with joy and great anticipation. My pastor husband and I embarked on our new life together, eagerly looking forward to the thriving ministry and big family that God would give us.

Although my faith never wavered, after three years of childlessness, our families, church members, and friends were asking us why we had no children. Many of them offered words of advice, and they had many questions we could not answer. Sometimes the pain of my barrenness seemed almost more than I could bear. But like Abraham and Sarah of old, we continued to pray and hope for a child.

One day a distant relative came to us with his family. He was dying of AIDS and asked if he and his family could stay for a while. Within a short time, our relative disappeared, leaving his family behind with us. Later we received word that he had died, and shortly after that, his wife left us also. Suddenly we found ourselves surrogate parents to three children.

Then a friend and his wife both became very ill, and it was soon discovered that both of them also were suffering from AIDS. That dreadful illness was quickly becoming an epidemic in our country of Uganda.

As many of our friends realized they were dying, they asked if they could come spend their last days with us. We took them in and cared for them until they died. Following the funerals, their children walked home from the burial grounds with us and became part of our family.

Almost before we comprehended what was happening, our

little parsonage became a refuge for terminally ill AIDS victims. Dying parents continued to appear at our door. We cared for them until they died, and then their children became our children. Soon our tiny home was overflowing. We kept adding small rooms with bunk beds. My mother moved into a little room at the back of our house to help care for the children.

Over the years, we became responsible for 22 children in all. Seventeen of them continue to live with us, as well as two mothers. Many of these children are AIDS orphans. As our "tribe" increased, we started a school in our church building. Later we were able to build a separate school building.

Now there are no longer tears of anguish and grief because of my barrenness. There's no time to cry. We're too busy caring for the children God has given into our care.

The joys and rewards continue. All of the children have accepted Jesus as Savior. They are preparing to be lawyers, nurses, teachers, pastors, and responsible leaders. All 17 of the children meet together at 6 A.M. each morning for Bible study and prayer led by two of our boys who have been called to preach.

Every day Nathan and I thank God for answering our prayers. We're so grateful that the Lord kept our faith steady through those years of emptiness. Truly He has filled our house with the laughter and shouts of our children. God has given us "exceeding abundantly" (Eph. 3:20, KJV) more than we could ask or think.

He has provided a house full—and running over!

🌾 **Lovincer Menya** *is a mother and pastor's wife. She works closely in ministry with her husband, Nathan. He is a district superintendent for the Church of the Nazarene in Uganda.*

20 ❦ Jean Oberlin

UNDER HIS WINGS

The dark, dusty closet enfolded me as I wrapped my arms around myself, rocking back and forth—waiting for the heroin high to kick in. As the familiar, warm rush flooded over me, I wondered why I ever expected anyone to love me when my own mother hadn't.

I was one of five kids. Throughout our childhood we were constantly shifted from place to place as our mother worked. We grew up without a father, but there was a man my mother brought home to live with us who molested me when I was between the ages of four and eight. Although my mother was aware of what he was doing, she did nothing to protect me. Her indifference hurt more than his abuse.

I started using drugs at an early age, and it numbed the pain for a brief time. But the more drugs and alcohol I used, the more it took to help me feel better. I was spiraling down into an endless cycle of despair. The men I chose were even worse off than I was, but somehow that made me feel better about myself. Pregnancy was never a concern, because I always managed to get the money together to just "take care of it." One morning at the clinic, and the pregnancy was behind me. The closet became my refuge—a place to escape to when my misery threatened to envelop me.

I married three times. I left one of my husbands with another woman—essentially trading him for drugs. One time a man put a gun to my head, demanding that I give him drugs. When he realized that I really didn't have any, he and I joined forces to search for a fix.

I learned to use my mother's guilt, which she felt because of her neglect of me when I was a child, to manipulate her into paying for my drugs. Even in the latter days of her life when she was dying from cancer, I relentlessly called her to go meet my dealer.

My last husband and I hid out in a rat-infested shack, living from day to day to supply our heroin and crack cocaine habits. Our whole lives centered around finding our next hit.

Another day as I walked down the railroad tracks near our one-room hovel, drunk and alone, a man came out of nowhere. He grabbed me, beat me in the face, robbed me, and threw me to the ground. As I lay there, I knew I needed help.

One night I was found unconscious, bleeding internally from an ulcer. It was the sixth time in four months that I was rushed to the hospital. All of the other times I had been hospitalized, my drinking buddies picked me up as soon as I was released, and in no time at all I was high again. But that night when I got to the hospital, the doctor told me that if I wanted to live I must never drink again.

I was sent to a treatment center upstate, and the people there were very kind to me. For three days they tapered down my drugs until the last day when I was "raw"—no drugs. It was the first time in 30 years of alcoholism and 24 years of heroin addiction that I was truly drug-free. I was so afraid. I remember going to my room and dropping on my knees. I cried out, *What am I going to do? God, help me!* Right then I felt a sense of peace settling over me. Somehow, I knew that God had heard my cry and was surrounding me with His love. That was July 17, 1995. From that day on, I knew I was being sheltered under His wings.

When I was released, everything felt different this time. I was surrounded by support at the halfway house where I lived, and I spent a year in a day program where I received care and encouragement. Many times I found bags sitting by my door that contained just what I needed. It was the first time in my life that I felt loved, and I even began to love myself.

Jean Oberlin

I eventually came to realize that it was time to get a job and stop collecting welfare. My sister Pat had accepted Christ and was praying for all of us.

I was still technically married to my third husband, Steve. He had contracted AIDS from sharing needles, and he still struggled constantly with his addictions, but we reconciled and moved into a small house. He was such a good man, but I was frustrated over and over by his continued drug use.

One day as I was walking up the hill to our home, I cried out, *God, if I could only find a good church where I could learn how to live for You!* Those words were barely out of my mouth when I looked into the weeds beside the road and saw a sign pointing to a church down the street. I quickly followed the directions and walked into the back door of the church. There was a service going on. I was dressed in my dirty work clothes, but I didn't let that bother me. I walked right down the center aisle to the front of the sanctuary. I knew people were looking at me and that I made them feel uncomfortable, and the service came to a halt. But Donna, the pastor's wife, came over to me and welcomed me warmly. She even hugged me! I felt the warmth of her love and acceptance. I knew this was where I belonged.

A few evenings later when I got home from my job, Steve came in, and I could tell he had been using heroin. Suddenly I was overwhelmed with the desire for that familiar rush. I ran into the bedroom and cried out to God for help.

The next morning Donna called me and asked, "What was going on with you at 11:00 last night? I woke up, and it was almost as though I could see you kneeling at the foot of our bed. So I prayed for you."

I cried out, *That's it! Lord, I surrender! God, save me!*

And He did.

The next Sunday morning the pastor announced that a baptismal service was being planned, and I signed up for it. In that service, as I stepped into the water it occurred to me that the date was January 17, 1996—one year to the day of sobriety! What a way to celebrate!

Today, when I think back to those dark days in the closet, I know that although they were lonely, fear-filled times, even then I was covered and loved. My loving Heavenly Father protected me and sheltered me—drawing me into the safe fold of His love.

🌿 **Jean Oberlin** *lives and works at a Christian conference center in upstate New York, where she serves the Lord, teaches Sunday School, and tells people about Jesus.*

21 ✺ Carol Rhoads

COMMITTED FAITH

As a teenager I promised God that I would serve Him in full-time Christian service. Because I spoke Spanish fluently, I expected the Lord to open the door for me to be a missionary in another country. I had faith that He would make His plans very clear, and I was committed to following His call, regardless of the cost.

During that period, I dated a popular basketball player for two years while we were students at Wheaton College. However, I became more and more disturbed by the fact that he did not have God's call on his life to full-time ministry, as I did. Repeatedly I tried to convince him that he could find fulfillment on the mission field. We began to argue constantly.

It never ceases to amaze me the measures the Lord goes to in order to get our attention. During a two-month period I was a passenger in three separate automobile accidents. Those mishaps caused me to refocus on God's call on my life, and my faith and recommitment to the Lord's plan for my life were solidified. I stopped dating the basketball player, and I immediately sensed heightened direction, great relief, and marvelous peace.

In God's perfect timing, the very next night after we broke up, Ross Rhoads and I had our first date. That was the beginning of a great partnership of faith and ministry that has resulted in 47 wonderful years of marriage.

For the first 18 years of our marriage, Ross was an evangelist, and we were thrilled with the joys of seeing many come to a saving knowledge of Christ. When Ross began to pastor, I came to realize the pressures and responsibilities of serving beside my husband in a local church. It was a blessing and privilege to serve as a pastor's wife for more than 20 years.

My life as a pastor's wife turned out to be more all-consuming than I had expected. Loneliness, insecurity, struggles, and overwhelming feelings of helplessness were constant challenges for me. But God's faithfulness and my strong faith and complete commitment to Him and our ministry helped me cope with the pressures.

One of the greatest challenges I faced was hearing undeserved criticism about my husband. Some of it was constructive, but there were instances when mean-spirited gossip hurt us deeply. When we felt tempted to just give up, we put our faith in God and reaffirmed our ironclad commitment to do whatever He asked of us.

Soon after I assumed the role of pastor's wife, I realized that some of the congregation had expectations of my role based on what the former pastors' wives had done. They began to drop not-too-subtle hints: "Our former pastor's wife headed vacation Bible school, another one taught the kids in the junior department, and our last pastor's wife had at least 20 people over for dinner every Sunday night." I felt overwhelmed.

Our children suffered from some identity problems of their own. One of them asked me, "If Daddy's called 'Pastor,' what do we call you?" They decided I should be "Mommy Pastor."

When I felt the stress and pressure intensifying and I felt uncertain of my role, I shared my concerns with Ross. His responses were always reassuring. He said, "Honey, you're the pastor's wife, not the church's wife." That wise statement provided more freedom for me than can be imagined.

Many people assume that pastors meet the needs of the church members ahead of the needs of their own families. I remember one Christmas morning in particular. We were just beginning to open our presents in front of our Christmas tree when the phone rang. A relative of a church member needed Pastor desperately and begged him to come.

Disappointed, the children and I moaned and groaned. I was a frustrated "Mommy Pastor" that morning, and I confess I aimed some unnecessarily sharp comments at Ross that made him feel guilty for leaving us. Torn, he ran out the door as he pulled on his coat. He ministered to their needs and hurried home so that we could finish opening our gifts. The interruption was soon forgotten.

Similar situations occurred many times during those years. Living in the glass walls of a parsonage was a constant challenge. But we were able to stay close to the Lord and to each other.

As our children grew and the church grew, the demands on me increased both at home and at church. Ross encouraged me to seek God's wisdom concerning how I to divide my time and responsibilities. He never pressured me to do what was expected.

Most pastors' wives are expected to attend prayer meeting, but there were many times when I sat at one of the children's ball games instead. Because I love to play the piano, I enjoyed playing for most of the services even when we starting having three Sunday morning services. But it became too much when the children had to wait through all of those services. I had to cut back.

Teaching our children the truths of God's Word and passing along our faith were fulfilling experiences. One of my greatest joys was teaching scripture to our children each week. They have learned thousands of verses, whole psalms, as well as Christmas and Easter passages and many more. We believed that God's Word planted firmly in their hearts and minds would equip them to live holy lives. Our two sons are now in ministry, and our daughter is a strong Christian. We thank God today that all three of our children and their spouses are growing in their walks with the Lord and are committed to instilling faith in their children's lives.

I was able to embrace my life as a pastor's wife because of my faith in God and His faithfulness to me. My faith has sustained me through the tough times. Because I have such a solid foundation, I have been protected from Satan's attacks of self-pity and discouragement.

One of my favorite verses is found in Eph. 6:10—"Be strong in the Lord, and in the power of his might" (KJV). Today I can say with great confidence that my commitment is stronger than ever. And my faith is unwavering, regardless of the difficulties and challenges I face. God is always faithful, and it's a joy to serve Him.

Carol Rhoads *is an accomplished pianist and former teacher. Her husband, Ross, is currently chaplain of the Billy Graham Evangelistic Association, special assistant to Franklin Graham, and vice chairman of Samaritan's Purse. They have three married children and 10 grandchildren.*

22 ✦ Ho Yeow Sun

SHINING FOR JESUS

When I was in secondary school, my English teacher introduced me to Christianity. She gave me a basic Bible study, and I learned about God. At that time I was battling depression and wondered if life was worth living. Through our studies I began to see that there was hope and joy in Jesus.

A few months after I started the Bible study, a stranger shared her testimony with me in a busy bus terminal. Although it was a strange place and time to do it, I bowed my head and prayed the sinner's prayer in the midst of all the noise and confusion of the bus terminal.

Not long after that, a handsome young pastor, Kong Hee, came to my school, and I rededicated my life to the Lord. I began attending the weekly cell group meeting he led. It was there that I felt God's call to enter full-time ministry. Kong Hee and I became copastors of the cell groups that were rapidly growing. After much prayer, in 1989 we stepped out on faith and purchased an old theater building and founded City Harvest Church.

Kong Hee and I served God wholeheartedly in the ministry. The thought of a relationship with him beyond friendship—much less marriage—was never discussed. But one day a friend and mentor advised Pastor Kong to settle down and get married.

It was an ordinary afternoon, and I was immersed in my work when he burst in. "Sun, let's get married!" There were no flowers, no diamond ring, no romantic ambience. Not exactly what I had thought a marriage proposal would be. But I knew it was right and that it was God's plan for our lives. The very next day we began to make wedding plans, and we were married six months later.

God's hand was on our marriage and our ministry from the very beginning. I began to sense His call to social work and pastoral ministry, so I enrolled in Bible school and subsequently graduated with a master's degree in pastoral counseling from a theological seminary.

In 1997 I felt led to found City Harvest Community Services Association (CHCSA). Our mission is to reach out to the less fortunate among us, regardless of race, language, or religion. We minister to the elderly, children, troubled youth, the terminally ill, the mentally handicapped, the hearing impaired, and prisoners. Each year we reach out to more than 4,500 clients, and CHCSA has become one of the largest social work agencies in Singapore.

One of my greatest blessings has been what the Lord has done with my musical talent. He has enabled me to become a recording artist under the Decca label. As I am privileged to perform concerts around Asia, God is blessing beyond measure. During concerts in Hong Kong and Taiwan, more than 15,000 souls were saved. One of those was a Triad leader over some 30,000 gang members. He came to my concert shortly after his release from prison, and he and his entire family accepted Jesus as Savior. A local pastor is mentoring and discipling them as they grow in Christ.

We have been blessed as the Lord has grown City Harvest Church from a small congregation of 20 to more than 13,000 members with a staff of 120. In early 2002 we moved into a new ministry center. Because of the faithful obedience of our people, our building will be debt-free by the end of 2003.

When I think back on what the Lord has done, I am so blessed that He has brought a troubled, hopeless teenager to this walk of faith. It is my greatest joy to see people come to know Jesus as Lord. My parents and other family members have become Christians as well.

Before I knew Jesus, I knew much darkness in my life, even though my name is Sun. But since the day the *Son* of God forgave

Ho Yeow Sun 83

my sins and came into my heart, His *Son*-light has been shining on my life.

Today I am a reflection of Jesus as I shine for Him!

 **Ho Yeow Sun** *is copastor with her husband, Kong Hee, of City Harvest Church in Singapore. She has a master of arts degree in pastoral counseling and cofounded City Harvest Community Services Association. She counsels dozens of individuals each month and hosts a radio call-in show. She is also an international recording artist under the Decca label with two double platinum albums.*

23 ✺ Natalie Ward

WRITTEN INTO GOD'S STORY

The tropical sun warmed me as I sat reading my Bible on the porch. I could hear a plane soaring overhead, the accompanying background noises of the birds in a nearby avocado tree, and the neighborhood children playing in the dirt road. As I leafed through my Bible, passage after passage reminded me again that my life journey of faith had been written into the story of God.

As I turned to Ps. 27 I could see reflections of God's faithfulness throughout my life written in the margins. Only a few lines of the whole passage were not underscored. Words were circled with arrows and dates indicating a particular time when God offered hope and confidence in Him through the Word. Written at the bottom of this passage I found "Be teachable, be strong, stand firm, in the Lord."

I was reminded of how my daily obedience was challenged when we accepted the position of field director for Melanesia. It was challenging to realize that we would be a family who lived one-third of the year separated from its spiritual leader—our husband and father—as he traveled away from home. It's a blessing to me now to recognize that the day-to-day obedience that made that possible was our firm foundation of faith in the One who asked this of our family.

My eyes were drawn to the words written in blue ink with the date April 15, 2002. I remembered the peace God gave me that day as I released my precious husband to travel once again into an area known for its criminal activity and extreme unrest. Through His faithful answers to my prayers, God had written me into His story.

Then I saw the date September 2, 2000, and read the words I had written in the right-hand margin. Once again I felt my burden for those in China who are lost in the worship of Buddha and evil spirits. My love for the Chinese people, my prayers for the believers there, as well as my broken heart for the lost were taken to a new depth on that day. For it was during that trip to China that I met a young Christian woman, a journalist. I admired her Chinese Bible with all its characters. To my surprise, she sweetly offered it to me as a gift! In that moment I knew God was asking me to give her my Bible, the precious one that my firstborn son had given to me when he was just 10 years old. God had known that a young journalist needed an English Bible to better reach the young people of China. So He had arranged our meeting and the exchange of Bibles. Once again, my life had been written into the story of God.

Above the words "hide me," I found the name of a national leader from Papua New Guinea whom we hid in our home when his life was threatened due to his brother's actions. His brother had been killed, and he was to be next. I bowed my head and whispered a prayer again for this precious man and his family. I asked that God would so fill our home with His presence that each one who enters would find the shelter of the Rock. I basked in the realization that my life is being written into the story of God.

The date April 4, 2002, caught my eye, along with the words "national elections." I remembered the fighting, killing, fear, burning, looting—and then the peace, comfort, confidence, goodness because of God's intervention.

My middle son's name is written in the margin by a verse I claimed for him. This tropical rain forest and its people have been home to him and his siblings since 1983. In just a few months he will graduate from high school and return to our homeland. It's an incredible comfort to know that as my children leave to live 10,000 miles away from me they are already written in God's story.

I wrote that day's date in the margin next to the words "even then will I be confident." I pictured my husband's travels through countries where the possibility of danger and the threat of terror are strong and the forgiveness of Christ's blood is not embraced. Just that morning, an upgrade in the security alert was given.

When I finished writing, an overwhelming peace flooded me. I have confidence and assurance that through my daily obedience, with my firm foundation of faith, God has a beautiful story—His story.

And I am written in it with His glorious hand!

🌿 **Natalie Ward** *is a missionary serving with her husband, Verne. He serves as the Melanesia field director overseeing ministries in Papua New Guinea, Solomon Islands, East Timor, and Vanuatu. They live with their children in Papua New Guinea.*

Section 3

Put aside all anxious thoughts and

imaginations

and say continuously,

"The Lord is my strength and shield."

—Francis de Sales

24 🌿 Joni Eareckson Tada

PRESENT-TENSE FAITH

I kept hearing the words over and over, "Have faith, Joni. One day it will all be better. You'll be OK."

I can't tell you how many times I heard similar statements from hurting friends and family who clutched the rails of my hospital bed in those first days and weeks after my injury.

They would say, "Have faith, Joni. Faith will keep you until the end."

Frankly, that sounded quite morbid to me.

There was no way I could ever be comforted by such words. Somehow, they made me think that nothing much was *really* ever going to change. As my life stretched ahead of me, I felt imprisoned by my paralysis. Faith appeared to be a hopeful, wishful desire—a religious warm fuzzy that I could embrace in that far distant future when somehow all of this would "make sense."

I didn't want to be a woman of great faith if it meant that I had to lounge around in a wheelchair the rest of my life hoping for pie in the sky. Now I realize that this whole idea is wrapped in a colossal misunderstanding.

As the Bible defines it, faith is not a past-tense "has been" concept. True faith represents present-tense action. It is accepting God's promises and taking action on them right now—*today!* The immediacy of the "right now" way of looking at God's promises is the essence from which the greatest people of faith are fashioned. They totally accept God at His word and live their lives based on those truths. For a true believer, faith is pulled out of the abstract, thrust from the nebulous nowhere, out of the inky twilight of uncertainty and lived out with concrete certainty in this present moment.

Somehow, somewhere in these years I came to fully realize that truth. It was on a lonely dark night in a sterile hospital room that the words of Heb. 11:1 began to permeate my stubborn defenses. At that moment I began to realize that faith means being sure of what we hope for—now. It means being confident that something is real, *in this present moment*, all around us, even when we cannot comprehend it or see it. And what is real? Jesus! Now and present.

When I truly started living like that I immediately understood that I could get a jump-start on heaven. I could start existing forever *today*. The absolute confidence that God's busy fingers were working on me and my life every moment of every day, even though I couldn't see them or feel them, flooded my being.

And I have proven it to be true. Great faith isn't possessing the ability to believe long and far into the uncertain future. Great faith comes through simply trusting God's Word *this moment*—and then taking the next step. It means holding fast to Jesus Christ, the Author and Finisher of our faith. And *that* is enough.

Adapted from Joni Eareckson Tada, *Glorious Intruder* (Portland, Oreg.: Multnomah Press, 1989). Used by permission.

Joni Eareckson Tada *is founder and president of JAF Ministries (Joni and Friends), an organization that accelerates Christian outreach in the disability community. Joni is a quadriplegic as the result of a diving accident in 1967. She is an internationally known speaker, author, and artist. She and her husband, Ken, live in Calabasas, California. Details about her life and ministry are available at www.joniandfriends.org.*

25 ❧ Renee Nolan

LOOKING FOR GOD ON THE 97TH FLOOR

Three-year-old Katie sang cheerfully along with her Veggie Tales tape as we pulled up in front of our dream house by the lake. Nestled in the vibrant foliage of late summer, the house and its setting were breathtaking. In just one more month our new home would be finished. My husband, Dan, and I and our two children could hardly wait to move in.

I got out of the car and walked around to unbuckle Katie's seatbelt. I was startled to see our builder's wife burst out of the front door, screaming incoherently. When I finally understood what she was telling me, my heart began to thud painfully in my chest. A hijacked airplane had crashed into one of the Twin Towers of the World Trade Center in New York City. Horrified, I began screaming, too, yelling, "Dan works there! *Oh, God—no. Please don't let it be!*" Poor little Katie began to cry at the top of her lungs. But in spite of our panic, none of us really comprehended how drastically our lives had changed.

We ran to a neighbor's house to find out more about what was happening. It seemed I was running in thick mud, and my body seemed to weigh twice as much as normal. I prayed to God that this was a horrible hoax.

But standing in front of the television set, I watched replays of the plane crashing into the side of the building, spewing forth a cloud of fuel and debris, and I could see that it was Dan's tower. As I watched the video over and over, I counted the floors. I collapsed onto my knees in anguish as I realized that the plane had impacted where Dan's office with Marsh, Inc., was located—on the 97th floor. I knew he was gone forever.

I cried, *God, where are You?* I found myself looking for Him, somehow expecting to see Him in the shadowy fireball, for I knew that only He could bring order from the chaos of the midair inferno. *God, are You there? Are You on the 97th floor?*

We had had such a great time that morning before Dan left for work. I'm not really a morning person, so it was unusual that I had gotten up with Dan a little after 5:00. As he ate Raisin Bran and drank coffee, I begged him to take the day off and stay home with us. There was an appointment at our new house that morning with the lender about our mortgage, and I wanted him to go with me. Using his special name for me, he kept saying, "Nay, you can do this! It'll be fine. Besides, I have a meeting. If you have any questions, just give me a call." We watched the news as he sipped his coffee. Then he gathered his things and leaned over the couch to give me a lingering upside-down good-bye kiss. I watched my 6'4, 245-pound, affable red-headed husband smile in his endearing gap-toothed way as he closed the door behind him. Just another day at the office.

The children were still asleep, so I reached for my Bible and read several verses and prayed the prayer of Jabez, as I did every day. Then I took a shower before awakening our seven-year-old son, J. D., for school. I hummed as I fixed his and Katie's breakfast. After the school bus pulled away, Katie and I followed the glistening lakeshore as we headed for our dream house. Little did we know that we were just minutes away from the most devastating tragedy of our lives.

How had such a brilliantly beautiful late summer morning turn into such a heart-wrenching nightmare?

With the help of the construction workers, I was finally able to load Katie in the car, and they drove us to our small rental cottage. I was in shock and disbelief as I called family and friends across the country. No one lived nearby, so I knew it would be hours before anyone arrived. Debbie, my builder's wife, is a strong person, and she stayed with me until the first of our family arrived. While we waited, we kept the television set on, and, because of nervous energy, I began to clean everything in sight. My neighbors began to arrive, and the nightmare began to feel real to me. I excused myself, saying I needed a shower. I went into the bathroom and turned on the shower, lost my stomach, and began crying to God. When I was in the shower I sobbed with a heart-wrenching pain only God could fathom. The Lord was with me in that shower, and I felt His comforting peace sweep over me. In a few minutes I was able to return to the outside world to wait for my family.

What an awful experience it was for everyone who came through my door that day! I waited by my phone to get any messages as family and friends gathered. Over and over we watched the smashing planes and the crumbling towers—along with the rest of the world.

As we watched for news on television and listened for the phone to ring, we began making lists of hospital numbers and other numbers to call. Every time the phone rang, my heart jumped into my throat as I clutched for a miracle. Could it be Dan? But I knew in my heart that he was gone. Family members brought kind and comforting words. They tried to convince me that maybe Dan had escaped or had been out of the office getting a bagel. That hope drove us during a four-day search filled with turmoil and grief.

When Dan's parents arrived, the pain intensified, but the Lord helped me comfort them, for they had lost their beloved son.

We set up a little command post at my tiny house. I'm thankful for the beautiful, cool weather that week, because many of those dear people had to sit outside. Everyone sheltered me from the television. Each night most of the family went to a nearby motel, while someone always stayed behind with the children and me. Even though we were all exhausted, they stayed up with me as I rambled on and on about Dan. During those sleepless nights I found myself listening for his footsteps on the porch or for him to pull up in his car any minute to tell me he was really OK.

We were informed through Marsh, Inc., that we needed to file a missing person's report. When they explained that I had to go into New York City to the Armory and stand in line with the mass of grieving people, I began to pray. I knew that was more than I could handle. Jason, Dan's cousin who lives in New York and knows his way around the city, volunteered for the job. He knew that he could call us on his cell phone to get any additional information he needed.

Jason later told me that when he arrived at the Armory, the scene was unbelievable. Grieving people were all around him, clutching pictures of loved ones and begging for any small amount of information. Jason patiently waited in long lines. He was on a mission, and he wanted to do everything he could to help me. He called a number of times to ask questions such as what color underwear Dan wore to work that day and if he was wearing any jewelry. Exhausted and in tears, Jason finally completed a detailed 12-page report. I cannot adequately express my gratitude to Jason for what he did for me.

On Thursday our chief of police from Hopatcong stopped by to check on us. He told me that I must go to the police station and file another missing person's report on Dan for the state of New Jersey. Although I felt like a zombie as I walked into the station, God gave me the strength to follow a very tall, gentle policeman into a room where he took my statement. This big man was in tears at the end of my report and assured me that he would do everything in his power to find Dan.

On Friday of that week, as we continued our daily ritual of meeting at the house, I asked Dan's mother, Eileen, if she thought Dan would come home. Through her tears she muttered the words, "No, Nay. Dan is not coming back." Everyone cried, and I felt the need to have closure that would allow the family to return to their own homes. All of us were tired and depressed and needed the comforts of home. So we decided to have a memorial service on Sunday to say good-bye to Dan. That gave us two days to call friends, coworkers, family members, and anyone we thought would want to come. We assigned tasks as we made plans for a loving memorial service at my church, First Baptist Church of Dover, New Jersey. Pastor John Hackworth was enormously helpful in taking care of the details.

On Saturday afternoon we had a birthday party with the family for Kaitlyn, who would be turning four on the 20th, since I knew I wouldn't be up to doing that alone. It was a good thing to do, and it brought our attention to a beautiful, smiling little girl who was excited about being four. When her party was over, Katie thought it would be good to send a balloon to Daddy in heaven. All the children drew pictures and wrote messages, and we sent the balloon sailing toward heaven. They were convinced that the balloon reached Dan somehow, and it made them smile.

My goal was to stay busy to keep from thinking. I knew that if I allowed myself to think, I would cry. For that week I existed in a state of numb shock. In retrospect, I know that God was with me and sustained me and kept me whole. Sunday we dressed and went to the church for the memorial service. I went in through the back to avoid contact with people and met up with Pastor Hackworth to pray. When it was time to go in to the service, I walked through the door to the auditorium and was amazed by the number of people who had come to express their love and say good-bye to Dan. I sat on the front row with my children and my parents. When I looked up at the platform, I saw a number of pictures of Dan that were arranged around numerous sprays of flowers. I began to cry as I looked at all those photographs, and the pain became overwhelming once again. They portrayed the Irishman we all knew and loved.

The service was brief and to the point. Robert, Dan's father, was somehow able to stand before everyone and speak of the son he remembered. The music was a sweet sound in my ears and comforted my soul. I had requested "It Is Well." The song was perfectly sung, reminding me that God was there and that it truly was well with my soul. After the service concluded, we went to the back of the church where a meal was provided for everyone. A long line formed as people gathered to give their condolences. I held onto a chair and hugged everyone who came by. My mother kept checking on me because she was concerned that I would collapse, but the Lord saw me through. Each time that I said good-bye to family and friends as they left to return their own homes, a part of me went with them, and I cried, feeling alone and vulnerable.

Early on Monday morning Dan's parents, my sister, Terri, and her son, Todd, and I boarded the train for New York City. We went to a large hotel that Marsh, Inc., had set up as its command post. Tragically, this insurance brokerage firm lost 297 employees on September 11. The company felt the need to give as much support as possible to its employees and their families. They had set up a room for the families with a wall of photos of missing persons where we could go and visit. They had also set up a room for human resources where I was able to find out what benefits Dan had and how my children and I would survive financially. A talented family sang spirituals in remembrance of its loved one. Every few hours the president and CEO of Marsh held a news briefing and answered questions from family members still looking for their loved ones. Every story was heartbreaking, and we heard many, many stories.

Though I still have many questions, I have the solace of my deep-seated faith in God's ability to sustain me. I find myself leaning day-to-day on the everlasting Rock of my salvation. As I have cried out to God time after time, I have unfailingly found rest and peace in the unwavering strong tower of my faith in Him.

And I have come to the full realization that, as incongruous as it may seem, God *was* there that day on the 97th floor!

Renee Nolan *is a gifted artist, speaker, and singer who enjoys working with interior designs. She and her children now reside in Wichita, Kansas.*

26 ✿ Joyce Williams

A HEAVENLY GLIMPSE OF MAMA

I was overwhelmed with sadness as the first Mother's Day without my own mother approached. I had lost Mama the previous August, and I was a thousand miles from my daughters, Tami and Beth. We had just received word that Uncle Lewis, Mama's brother and the patriarch of our family, was dying of cancer. It was not possible for me to be with any of them, and my heart was heavy.

I remembered how the Lord comforted me the day Mama died. The call had come on Sunday morning—Mama was gone. I was so far away, and Gene and I couldn't get a plane out until the next day. So I spent the afternoon and evening going through belongings of Mama's that I had with me.

I was flooded by memories. Mama was unstintingly unselfish. I remember her taking my sister Jane and me shopping. When she could, she took us to Heironimus, one of the nicest stores in town. At great personal sacrifice, she bought us matching outfits, although I don't remember her ever buying anything for herself. That was just the way Mama was.

As I sorted through a box I found an envelope that I didn't remember seeing before. Her spidery handwriting brought fresh tears to my eyes. But the words I read lifted my heart.

Mama had always said her favorite song was "Beulah Land" as sung by my daughter, Beth. So I was surprised to read, "My favorite songs are 'It Is Well with My Soul' and 'I'd Rather Have Jesus.'" That sums it up, doesn't it? When our lives are over and we have a final testimony to leave as a legacy of our faith, those words say it all.

As I reflected on the way the Lord had brought such comfort

when Mama died, I was assured that He would find a special way to console us as we walked back through the valley when Uncle Lewis passed away.

On Friday I called my cousin, Patsy. She said that Uncle Lewis's death was imminent. He had almost died on Wednesday night but had somehow rallied. As a matter of fact, he had been so much better that the doctor sent the family home to rest around midnight.

Patsy went on to tell me that early Thursday morning his nurse, a family friend, heard Uncle Lewis mumbling. She paused for a moment and listened. Then she moved closer to his bed. Leaning toward him, she heard him say, "It's much more beautiful over there than I ever dreamed. Look at all the angels! There's a big river, and I can see lots of people on the other side." He paused and then said, "I see Mary!" Then he drifted back into unconsciousness. When Patsy finished, I couldn't speak because I was so overcome with emotion. He had seen Mary, his sister— Mama! Uncle Lewis was given a glimpse of heaven and that very special resident. I felt such joy! What a Mother's Day gift— straight from heaven!

Patsy called early Saturday morning to tell me that Uncle Lewis had joined Mama. Rather than the sorrow I was anticipating, I was comforted with the thought of Mama welcoming him. Imagine—my humble mother as a heavenly greeter! I visualized brother and sister exploring heaven together in their new bodies. I pictured them walking on streets of gold, hand in hand, shouting joyfully. I'm sure Daddy was holding Mama's other hand as they helped reacquaint Uncle Lewis with so many of his family and friends who had gone ahead.

One of my favorite memories of Mama was of her reading her big black Bible. Most of the time it was opened to Rev. 21 as she read over and over about heaven.

That Mother's Day was a joyous celebration rather than a sad farewell.

27 ❧ Joyce Williams

FAITH ON HER KNEES

My younger sister, Jane, and I have always adored our big sister, Bobbi. She is so much fun, and we love hanging out with her. Although she was in an abusive marriage and life was tough for her, we still had fun when we were together.

Over the years I've called Bobbi when I really need help. There's never a job too menial or a task too difficult for her. My big sister always listens and responds, gladly doing what needs to be done.

As with our mama, Bobbi's favorite place is in the back of the crowd, the last pew in the church. She never seeks to draw attention to herself as she quietly soaks up the music and message of the day.

It seems that difficulties have plagued Bobbi each step of her way. But she always finds a way to get through each day by holding onto her faith in God to sustain and guide her.

I remember calling her one day when my daughter Beth was desperately sick with a lupus flare-up. When I told Bobbi how critical Beth was, she said, "I'm going to stop everything I'm doing and pray right now." Later she told me that she fell to her knees right there in her living room and cried out for God to touch Beth. And He did! Once again, Beth stabilized.

There's no way to describe what it means to have a big sister who is a great woman of faith. Although she has been battered by many storms, her faith has never been shattered. The only time she's down is when she's on her knees before God. And He continues to reward her by lifting her up and guiding her through the storms.

28 ❧ Joyce Mehl

THE GOOD FIGHT

It was a rare day in Portland—one of those blue-sky days, the kind you'd like to bottle up and keep for the long weeks of rain and gray skies that are sure to follow.

As Ron and I walked through the parking lot into the clinic, we had no idea that the light and warmth of that beautiful day were about to be eclipsed.

Inside, settled into chairs in David Regan's office, it was obvious that our dear friend and oncologist was choosing his words carefully. He had the results of Ron's bone marrow biopsy in his hand—the tests he had ordered to determine why Ron's red and white blood cell and platelet counts had plunged to almost zero.

The biopsy revealed that the bone marrow was packed with leukemia cells—rendering the marrow incapable of producing healthy cells. It was clear, then, that the leukemia we had battled for years had reached a critical pass. But that wasn't all. "Ron," David went on to say, "the biopsy also tells us that your leukemia is no longer responding to the chemotherapy treatments."

No longer responding? It was very quiet for a moment, and then hesitantly I spoke up: "If the chemotherapy isn't working anymore, what are the other options?"

"There is one treatment that is so new that there's very little data available on patient response," David said, looking up at us. "It's a very hard treatment with potentially challenging side effects. It compromises your immune system, leaving you even more vulnerable to infection than you already are. Because of that, Ron, if you choose this treatment, you'll be in virtual isolation for four months, and you'll be extremely fatigued. There are no guarantees that it will even work. But from what we know, it looks very promising for the future."

I didn't hear David's last sentence. All I could think about were his words "hard treatment" and "challenging side effects." Hadn't things been hard and challenging enough? How much more could Ron take? How much more could all of us take?

Ron broke the silence. "David, what if I *don't* do this? What if I don't take the treatment? How long would I have? Months? Years?"

David's eyes seemed to avoid ours for a moment. "Well," he answered softly, "I'd say about two months."

I felt a sudden desperation. Tears stung my eyes. I thought about our marriage, of our two boys and their families, our precious grandchildren, the dear people we had pastored for nearly 30 years. All our plans and our dreams for the future.

We left the office that day with many unanswered questions. But as we cried out to the Lord together, seeking His will, He began to reveal himself to us and show us the path He wanted us to walk.

Ron was to take the treatments. We knew that much. And after that? Well, the Lord would simply take care of our "after thats" just as He always has.

It was during this season of our lives that I found myself beginning to understand a little of what Paul might have meant when he told young Timothy, "Fight the good fight of faith" (1 Tim. 6:12, KJV). When Paul spoke those words, he knew what it meant to get a negative report. He had experienced the darkness of the dungeon. More than once, he had received the sentence of death. After being shipwrecked, he had spent endless hours tossed about in the cold, black waters of the sea.

Yes, Paul knew what it meant to fight the good fight of faith.

One thing I've discovered about this fight—it's different from any other. In most battles, you fight to win. In the fight of faith, you win through surrender. A life of faith must be a life of full surrender—surrendered to *all* the Father's plans—whether we like them or not, whether we understand them or not.

Even so, there are times when I would very much like to control my own circumstances. One day I asked my three-year-old granddaughter, Liesl, if she would like to go to the mall and ride the train (the kind you put a quarter in that just bumps around in one spot and never goes anywhere). When she said yes, I asked if we should take her little brother, Warner, along. "Sure," she chirped. "He can be the passenger, and I can be the driver—because I really like to be in control!"

I know just what she means. Bumping along down the rails of life can be very frustrating when you have no control, no way of accelerating or braking. But I've also learned that my very attempts to *gain* such control are what cause so much of the bumping around!

A life of faith is a life of trust, not control. Isa. 40:14 says, "Has the LORD ever needed anyone's advice? Does he need instruction about what is good or what is best?" (NLT).

Can I really offer the Creator and Lord of everything counsel about what I need? Should I make a list for Him, telling what would be good or what would be bad for me or those I love? Jesus tells us, "Your Father knows the things you have need of before you ask Him" (Matt. 6:8, NKJV).

Surrender becomes a little easier when I remember all He's done for me.

"What then shall we say to these things? If God is for us, who can be against us? He who did not spare His own Son, but delivered Him up for us all, how shall He not with Him also freely give us all things?" (Rom. 8:31-33, NKJV).

I'm not afraid to release all that concerns me to the One who loves me so much. In fact, *all* of God's purposes are wrapped in His love. His greatest purpose of all is to make me more like Him. Is there any way that could be bad?

I am privileged to live with a man who is not afraid to face

Joyce Mehl

dark days—days of great physical pain and intense emotional disappointment. In all these times, he has never complained or questioned God. And I know the reason he hasn't is because of the total surrender of his life to Jesus along with his great faith in Him as the faithful Caretaker of all he has surrendered.

The word "surrender" is used in 1 Cor. 13:3—and there it means "to give" or "sacrifice."

Jesus gave His life. He sacrificed His life. You could even say He surrendered. And He won!

Joyce Mehl *is a writer and speaker. She works closely with her husband, Ron, in ministry. He is senior pastor of Beaverton Foursquare Church in Beaverton, Oregon.*

29 ❦ Buay Tan

RESTORING THE BROKEN VESSEL

"I'm sorry—we've tried our best," the doctor uttered coldly and mechanically. These were the usual words of doom repeated at all deathbeds. But this time they were exclusive to Kim San and me. The doctor was pronouncing the death of Boon, our 19½-year-old son. I was stunned, stone dead. Desperately and at a loss for words I turned to Kim San and cried, "Boon is gone!"

When the business of bereavement and burial was over three days later, our walk "through the valley of the shadow of death" commenced with pain beyond description. We were in a living hell. A mysterious sense of trepidation, timidity, and tremors gripped us. There was no way of escape. It was always with us—in our waking hours, in our sleep, in our dreams, and in our nightmares.

Fearful of the suddenly cold world around me, I sought refuge in a small room in the church. It became my haven of isolation and seclusion for four solid months of mourning and misery. The outside world ceased to exist for me as I was totally immersed in grief, wrestling with my pain, oblivious to everything else.

In addition to our own individual struggles, Kim San and I tried to share each other's burdens—making sure that the other was all right. Yet we knew that we were not all right. The most traumatic moments were mealtimes, when we forced food down our throats and then struggled to keep it down. We were reluctant to go home in the evenings because our home was saturated with a strong sense of stillness without Boon. Nights became nightmares as Kim San struggled to sleep. My pillow was soaked with tears as I cried incessantly. Sleep eluded me for months.

Each morning brought despondency and despair. Kim San braced himself to go to church to counsel, preach, teach, and arrange funerals for others. As we lived through each day, we were constantly reminded of the doctor's doomsday prognosis: "You need time for your grief. Sometimes it takes years." Years? We could barely face each day.

My daily nourishment came from the Bible and from hymns. I searched the scriptures constantly for sustenance. But even familiar passages brought little comfort. Ps. 23 has always been meaningful to many people. But when I read it, the portion that hit me hardest was "Surely goodness and mercy shall follow me all the days of my life" (v. 6, KJV). I was incensed because of the irony and sarcasm of it. A deep sense of treachery overwhelmed me. It could not be true! How could God's promise hold true for me? Nothing good and merciful could come to Kim San and me from Boon's death.

But at the same time, the verse "as the heavens are higher than the earth, so are my ways higher than your ways, and my thoughts than your thoughts" (Isa. 55:9, KJV) kept coming to mind. I did not understand why God blessed us with Boon and then took him back so soon.

Boon had such a promising future. He was intelligent, gifted, and full of compassion and generosity for everyone. He was a talented artist, musician, historian, actor, computer expert, chef, and scholar and could discuss any topic at length. I cannot imagine the marvelous things that Boon would have accomplished if he had been given more time.

Deep in my heart I wondered, *Dear Lord, do You know what we've lost?* I felt like a vessel that had been shattered to pieces. An earthen vessel has no soul or spirit, and once broken, that's the end of it. But this vessel has an extremely fragile and delicate spirit. Even after it's broken, the spirit and pain linger on. In my grief the only way out for me was death. The pain was excruciating, and the struggle was suffocating. When I finally reached my lowest point, I thought that if I could not die and be with Boon, then my faith in the Lord had to be restored in order to keep on living. After all, He is the giver of life.

Gradually, in a very gentle and mysterious way, He answered my cry of agony and desperation. He renewed my faith and showed me how to trust Him absolutely again. I knew that my strength and hope depended on my faith in the Lord.

Since I had no choice but to carry on living, I decided to be better, not bitter; to be faithful, not fearful; to win and witness for Him, not whine and whimper. Once again, the Lord became my friend instead of my foe. I knew that was what Boon would have wanted as well.

When I finally changed courses, things began to get a little better. The Lord honored my renewed faith and began to restore my strength and confidence a little each day. He enabled me to write two manuscripts and opened a door for me to teach in an international school. He is leading many people into my path so that I can share His passion even in my pain.

My merciful and loving God has heard my cry. He has taken away my fear of living without Boon. As He continues to restore me to physical and spiritual health, He is slowly but surely piecing together this broken vessel.

🌾 **Buay Tan** *is an English language specialist/linguist and published author. She has taught for more than 23 years and is also a gourmet chef. She works alongside her pastor husband, Kim San, in ministry at the Church of Singapore.*

30 ✻ Joyce Rogers
THE VALLEY OF THE SHADOW

I was in the Judean desert in the area known as the Valley of the Shadow of Death. One particular deep, narrow valley is especially treacherous. As I looked through the zoom lens of my camera, I could barely see a flock of sheep coming through that pass. Although the terrain is very dangerous, the sheep followed their shepherd with total faith in his ability to lead them.

My mind flashed back many years ago to a happy Sunday afternoon. It was Mother's Day. We had just finished lunch, and I was headed to my bedroom to rest. I passed by our little baby Philip's bed and glanced in at him as he napped. But he looked very strange. Something was dreadfully wrong. I called for my husband, Adrian, to come quickly. Horrified, I asked, "Is he dead?"

Adrian quickly picked up his little body and tucked him in inside his coat. He said, "You stay here." Our other children were napping, and he didn't want to alarm them. Adrian rushed out to the car and drove as fast as he could to the hospital.

While he was gone, I was there alone with God. It seemed that I was walking through my valley of the shadow of death. My faith sustained me as words came to my mind and heart that I had memorized as a child. Looking toward heaven, I prayed Ps. 23. Then I came to those awesome words:

"Yea, though I walk through the valley of the shadow of death, I will fear no evil: for thou art with me; thy rod and thy staff they comfort me" (v. 4, KJV).

Those words took on a new meaning for me. "For thou art with me." In that stark moment I felt His presence.

And then I saw Adrian coming up the walk empty-handed. I

knew Philip was gone—gone to be with Jesus. I had been thrust into the Valley of the Shadow of Death, but Jesus walked with me. He never left my side. Without His presence, the pain in my heart would have been unbearable.

Following Philip's death, I began to dig deeper into God's Word and to lean hard on Jesus. He showed me many promises, and the words of Ps. 63:3-4 became my life verses.

"Because thy lovingkindness is better than life, my lips shall praise thee. Thus shall I bless thee while I live: I will lift up my hands in thy name" (KJV).

Frankly, I didn't feel like praising God. But by faith I began to claim this promise, to lift my hands to God and praise Him. After some time there came the day when I realized that I felt like praising God.

In an entirely different situation, Jesus once again walked with me and gave me great comfort. I was returning from Spain where I had visited our missionary son, David, and his family. As I boarded the plane, it began to snow unexpectedly, and we were delayed for the plane to be deiced. Consequently, when I arrived in Amsterdam I missed my connecting flight.

I found myself alone in a strange country until the next day. It was suggested that I take a bus to a hotel. As I walked through the shops in the airport headed toward the bus stop, I was suddenly enveloped by an overwhelming sense of loneliness.

Once again, my faith sustained me as I remembered Ps. 23. As I walked, I prayed the words out loud to the Lord. I told Him, *Lord, I feel so alone, but You promised that You're my Shepherd and that I would not want for anything. Lord, You said that You would give me peace— that You would make me to lie down in green pastures and lead me beside still waters. Because of Your name, You have pledged to restore me and lead me in the right way. Lord, You know that I love Your name. You know that I have walked through the valley of the shadow of death. You helped me not to fear. You were there to protect and comfort me. I know You will guide and help me now. Yes, You have even promised a bountiful banquet when enemies*

surround me. I believe You when You said that goodness and mercy will follow me every day and that I can look forward to living with You forever.

It was at the moment I finished praying Ps. 23 that I looked up and saw the missionary parents I met before I boarded the plane. They exclaimed, "We were looking for you!"

I replied, "Oh, praise the Lord! He answers prayer in such unexpected ways!" They invited me to ride the bus to the hotel and eat dinner with them. We had a lovely evening.

I called Adrian to tell him what had happened. Then I laid my head on the pillow and rested my soul on the promises of my Good Shepherd. He had assured me that He would be with me, to lead and protect me, to comfort me. He kept His promise.

Because our luggage had stayed at the airport, I purchased a toothbrush at the front desk. It was right after Christmas, and they still had a few tree ornaments decorated with Dutch artwork, so I bought one. Each Christmas I hang it on our tree as a reminder of the evening I spent with my Good Shepherd.

So as I continue to watch that shepherd lead His flock through the Valley of the Shadow of Death, I pause to thank my Good Shepherd for leading me so faithfully. I know that regardless of where He directs me, because of my faith in Him and the reality of His promises, He will guide me safely home.

I will never be alone—even in the Valley of the Shadow of Death.

Joyce Rogers *is a homemaker and pastor's wife. She works alongside her husband, Adrian, who pastors Bellevue Baptist Church in Memphis. Joyce is a speaker, singer, a leader of women's ministries, and an author. She and her husband have four grown children, who are all active in Christian service.*

31   Jeanne Stucky

THE STRENGTH OF THE LORD

As I drove to Duke University Hospital that day, I admit that my faith was a little shaky. I had lots of questions and doubts, and I found that the driving time was a perfect opportunity for extended communication with the Lord.

For years, my husband, John, had been the strength and conditioning (weight lifting) coach for the University of Tennessee. He had always been very strong, robust, and extremely health-conscious. So as a family we were totally unprepared for the changes John had experienced physically and cognitively over the last two years.

It was obvious to everyone that John's job has always been his ministry. He referred to the athletes he worked with as his "puppies," praying for them, counseling them, and leading all who would listen to the Lord Jesus. It broke our hearts when this once strong man could no longer walk unassisted because of balance problems. His speech became slurred, he lost his short-term memory, his vision became impaired, and he began experiencing mental confusion. This once-mighty warrior for the Lord became a shadow of the person our son, Philip, and I had always known and loved.

I remembered studying about Elijah when he felt as if the heavens were sealed, and his prayers were getting nowhere. The flame of my faith was barely flickering. Oh, I had lots of questions!

John had already undergone two brain stem surgeries in less than a year. The lengthy two-year process of getting a diagnosis for a rare brain stem compression called Arnold Chiari Malformation, had physically and emotionally battered our family. Feeling as though the heavens were closed to my prayers for my husband, I continued to pray with quiet desperation as we drove to Duke University Hospital for his neurological examination.

As I drove along the interstate highway, suddenly our car hydroplaned and began moving out of control toward the back of a flatbed tractor-trailer that had stopped in front of us. I thought, *We're going to die!* and quickly prayed, *Lord, be with our son if we die today. Please, Jesus—help us!* It seemed as if we were heading toward that flatbed in slow motion. I had been crying out to God all the way from Knoxville for answers and His protection. I began screaming, *Lord, are You listening? Do You hear me, Jesus? Do You care?*

Our car was racing toward that flatbed tractor-trailer as though it had been shot out of a cannon!

Was God there? Yes! And He showed me in a mighty way. We hit the truck and came to an abrupt halt. I was fine. But I was immediately afraid the car might catch fire or explode because we had a full tank of gas. We were wedged under the truck. I could get out, but the emergency people and I couldn't get John to move or respond to our questions. They told me that he appeared to be severely injured. I cried out to God, *Lord, I know this is a stupid prayer because they're telling me that John is badly hurt. But please, Lord— help him to live and to be uninjured!* I knew that I could not live with the guilt that something happened to John while I was driving. He was pinned in the car, and his injuries looked horrific.

The firemen and paramedics requested that a medical helicopter be sent to the accident site. They had closed the interstate, and I thought it was too late for God to answer my prayer. About 15 minutes later, John was cut out of the car, and both of us were taken to a small hospital nearby. Glass had cut my hands, but all I needed were a few stitches. John's glasses had been broken by the car's airbag, so he had a few cuts on his face and bruises on one leg where the car engine was pushed into the passenger area.

God answered what I thought was an impossible, stupid prayer. Upon closer examination, John didn't appear to be severely injured. However, because of his previous brain stem surgeries, the hospital had the medical helicopter take him to Duke University Hospital. Policy would not allow me to go with John in the helicopter. There I was, stuck three hours from Duke, my car totaled, and I didn't know how I would get to John.

Then God showed me that He was in control. He cared and was providing beyond our wildest expectations. In the emergency room of that small hospital a lady I had never met named Gaye walked in and asked for Mrs. Stucky. When I said, "I'm Mrs. Stucky," she told me that the Lord had sent her to give me a ride to Durham, North Carolina (where Duke University Hospital is located). My sagging faith was incredibly strengthened through this wonderful woman who had been sent by God to minister to me.

On our way to Durham, I experienced God's love through Gaye. She told me that her husband owned the towing company that took our car and explained that the roads had become extremely slick that day from a light drizzle. Because the area had been without rain for such a long time and oils had built up on the roads, the slippery conditions had caused other accidents with fatalities. She explained that if we had hit the flatbed a little more to the right or a little more to the left, both of us would have been decapitated. The helicopter had been called because the wreck was so terrible, and they were sure that even if we survived we would be severely injured. Gaye took me to Durham, encouraging me, praying with me, ministering to me—much like the ravens did for Elijah. That day, I realized the heavens were not closed to my prayers, and God was in control.

Our medical odyssey was not yet over. John underwent two more brainstem operations and three shunt surgeries. Today the doctors say John's symptoms manifest themselves like those of Alzheimer's disease or dementia.

Philip and I have prayed for John's complete restoration,

always ending with, *Not our will, but Thine*. God's answer is *I am sovereign*. He continues to show us His love, His care, and His strength on a daily basis. Our Heavenly Father continues to give us a special love for John even though he is not the man we have known. God gives us His strength to be in a family where the spiritual leader is no longer leading. He has shown us He can take care of our needs. He has provided for every financial need, big and small. Philip has a full scholarship for college. Our family has been provided disability and in-home nursing care. God has provided me with a part-time job.

Is this what I wanted? No! I'm not a saint, and I don't always appreciate the hard times that have come my way. However, they have brought me closer to God. There are days when I lose my patience and temper when my husband gets confused, forgets he has eaten, thinks night is day, and does not sleep. Is God there for me on those days? Absolutely. He is patient with me, grants me forgiveness when I ask, and gives me His strength for the next day.

John loved the ministry God gave him. He was one of the top three weightlifting coaches in the nation when his disabilities forced his retirement. Over the years he watched God change the lives of many young men. His dream of coaching at the University of Tennessee with Phillip Fulmer was fulfilled. John raised a godly son. So while many people look at us and say how sad it is that God has not answered our prayers or healed John, I know that this is not true, because we're not at the end of our story. One day the Lord Jesus will give John a new body, either on earth or in heaven. As for me, He has brought me to the place where I don't question or doubt, because I know He is sovereign. I continuously find His grace to be sufficient for each day.

We thank God for the foundation of faith that came from years of committed Christian living, prayer, and Bible studies. We were coached by the Strength Trainer of the universe! Just as all of John's years of conditioning and training as strength and

Jeanne Stucky   115

conditioning coach for the University of Tennessee prepared the team, God has been getting us ready for these challenging years.

Today we can affirm that our greatest lessons have been learned through exercising our faith in the Lord to carry, guide, and guard us wherever life's game plan takes us. How comforting to know that regardless of the outcome, we're on the winning team!

Jeanne Stucky *is a homemaker. Since the illness of her husband, John, she has worked in a variety of positions that have enabled her to care for him. She is involved in Bible Study Fellowship and is developing a ministry to families with members who suffer from chronic illness. Jeanne and John live in Knoxville, Tennessee. Their son, Phillip, is a college student.*

Section 4

My heart has trusted in Him,

He has forgiven me, and I am helped.

He is not only with me but in me,

and I am in Him.

—Francis de Sales

.

32 ❦ Joyce Williams

TRANSPLANTED MEMORIES

"Hey, Pops! What are you gonna do about Mama's tree?" As we watched the twinkling Christmas lights, Pat and his dad, then my husband of four years, were reminiscing. My immediate thought was *What tree? I didn't even know we had a Mama's tree.* Later that evening, as the fading embers in the fireplace sparkled and popped, I asked Gene to explain.

He took my hand, and we walked to the door. As he pointed to the lovely crabapple tree out front, he told me its story. When his first wife, Bettye, died unexpectedly almost six years earlier, their wonderful neighbors had wanted to provide a special memorial. So they got together, selected that tree, and planted it in her memory. Every time the family came home, the tree's branches waved a welcome reminding them of their dear mother. Gene's story intensified my love for that circle of neighbors.

We were moving into a new house in just a few weeks, so Pat was justifiably concerned about what would happen to his mother's tree. Much love was planted there along with that crabapple tree. I put my mind to work. Then it came to me. I knew that somehow I must find a way to move that tree to our new lawn!

It was a tough last Christmas season in that house for Gene's children and grandchildren. In some ways they were saying good-bye to their mother again. This had been her dream house, and it was the last place they had seen her alive. I had been searching for months for a way to transfer their mother's memory to our new home so they would feel that a part of her was also there to greet them when they came to visit. This tree was the perfect thing! If I could have that tree transplanted, then maybe they would feel comfortable in our new home.

On Monday morning after Gene left for the office, I called Larry and Carol, our realtors. When I told them of my idea, they immediately became coconspirators. That day they began a search to find a tree to replace the one out front. I called Ilsik, the landscaper for our new house. He also was captivated by the idea, and a "deep rooted" collaboration began to take shape.

As spring approached, our new house was completed, and we began to make plans to move. Larry and Carol sneaked over to the house late one afternoon and hid the replacement tree deep in the bushes beside the house. I took several pictures of what I now called "Mama's tree." A few days later, Ilsik and his crew came with a huge tree-mover and began digging. I found myself humming in the kitchen as I prepared dinner, keeping time with the equipment out front.

A few minutes later, my tune was interrupted by the jangle of the doorbell. Hastily I dried my hands and went to the door. Ilsik stood there with dismay written all across his face. He said, "Joyce, I can't believe it, but this tree's root system is decaying. Come look." When he brushed the dirt from the gnarled, rotting, and twisted roots, even I could see that there were major problems. Then he said, "I'm not sure that there's anything we can do to salvage this tree. It's dying. What should I do? Do you want me to try to treat it and go ahead with the move? I don't think it will survive, but it's up to you."

Without a moment's hesitation I responded, "Yes! We've got to go ahead!" The tree surprise had become an obsession with me. We just had to try! I had faith that God would restore that tree. After all, we had nothing to lose. Ilsik said the tree would die in a couple of months if we left it. So he and his men carefully wrapped the diseased roots and loaded the crabapple tree onto his truck. Then after treating the soil, he quickly planted the new tree in the hole.

After dinner that evening I took Gene by the hand and walked with him out to the new tree. When I told him of our

  Joyce Williams

conspiracy, tears glistened in his eyes. I could see that he was touched by the thoughts of what this would mean to the family.

Ilsik planted that dying old crabapple tree in the most visible corner of our new yard. It would be the first thing people saw when they pulled into our driveway. I had never heard of anyone making house calls for an ailing tree, but Ilsik did! Day after day he nurtured and babied the crabapple tree with special chemicals and nutrients, saying, "I'm not sure this is going to work, but we'll keep trying." He propped it up with stakes and strong cords for support. For the first time in my life I prayed for a tree!

Early one morning just before moving day I drove to our new house. I had gotten into the habit of checking out our sick tree as I drove into the driveway. To my amazement, I saw that something was different. Hastily I flung open the door and raced over to the tree. Tight little buds dotted the branches! It was still alive! I could hardly wait for Gene to see it.

Our first Sunday in our new home was Easter. After church the family came for dinner. I handed each family member a large Easter card along with a picture of "Mama's tree" in front of the old house. Then I invited them to go outside to see the tree's new location. Their surprise was the only reward I needed.

A few weeks later, son Brent and his family were standing out front with me, and we were admiring their mama's tree. As I looked closer, I was amazed to see that not only were the leaves healthy and full, but there were new green shoots spiking up out of the ground near the trunk of the tree. Joyously we hugged each other.

Each spring as the pink blossoms erupt from the burgeoning dark green foliage, that crabapple tree grows taller and wider. Its branches are waving wands that weave a windy Kansas welcome to all who come. I'm so glad that this special memory survived and our faith was rewarded. Now every year we gather new leaves for our thriving scrapbook of transplanted memories.

33 🌿 Oreta Burnham

FAITH ENOUGH TO GO BACK

The jangling telephone jolted us from deep sleep at 2 A.M. Groggily, I groped for the phone and muttered, "Hello." Someone asked for Paul, and I handed the phone to him. His attention was immediately riveted to the call as one of our mission leaders told him that Martin and Gracia, our son and daughter-in-law, had been abducted by unknown kidnappers. He told Paul what they knew at that point and instructed him to go to the Internet and read more about it. When Paul hung up the phone, I asked, "Who was that? What's going on?" When he finally told me, I couldn't believe it. It just didn't seem real. Things like abductions happened to other families—not ours.

Our son Martin had just left our Kansas home two days earlier to return to the Philippines, where he and Gracia served as missionaries. He was a pilot who flew supplies to missionaries all around the country. It had been a blessing to have him with us as he updated us on the work. We had spent more than 30 years in the Philippines working as teachers and church planters among the Ibaloi (e-ba-loy) tribal people. In the last few years we were involved in translating the Old Testament scriptures into the Ibaloi language. Paul and I had returned to the states for a few months to complete some paperwork. We were looking forward to returning to our assignment.

During his brief visit with us, Martin hadn't told us anything about planning to go to the Dos Palmas island resort. We found out later that Gracia had arranged the surprise once-in-a-lifetime getaway to celebrate their 18th wedding anniversary. When Martin arrived back in the Philippines, she had planned every detail and whisked him off for a second honeymoon that quickly turned into their worst nightmare.

Anxious for news, we explored the Internet and gathered information throughout the nights and days to come. We learned that near daybreak on Sunday morning, May 27, 2001, terrorists with machine guns and other weapons took over the resort and abducted 17 vacationers and 3 resort personnel, forcing them into a waiting boat. Our concern mounted as we pictured Martin, Gracia, and the other captives at sea and at the mercy of ruthless militants.

As word spread, prayer began to circle the globe, and we were sustained by our faith in God's goodness. Immediately we felt the steadying calm of God's grace as He held us through each stage of the mounting crisis. We were convinced that this was a short-term situation and that our loved ones would be released soon. We were absolutely convinced that God was in control and watching over them, and we prayed for wisdom for those who were handling the negotiations. Our concern intensified when word came that they had been taken into the dense jungle from a hospital where the military had surrounded them. We assumed that negotiations would take place at the hospital for their release. We knew that this new development would make rescue efforts much more difficult.

As parents we are extremely blessed. Each of our five children has a close walk with the Lord, and four of them are missionaries. Growing up with the tribal people, loving them, and sensing their need for Jesus, they each responded to God's call. Our daughter Cheryl and her husband, Walt, were serving several hours away. When she got word of the kidnapping, they and their five children went immediately to be with Martin and Gracia's three children, Jeff, Mindy, and Zach. As the days stretched into weeks, we began to realize that this was turning into a prolonged situation. So Cheryl and Walt packed the children's things, and they all flew to stay with us at our home in Kansas.

As we embraced our grandchildren, our hearts were melted with love, and we determined to care for them as Martin and Gracia would. We did our best to comfort and reassure them. They had left behind their parents, friends, and their country. Their schooling had been disrupted. Although they were angry with the rebels for taking their parents, they wanted to go back "home." Slowly they adjusted as best they could.

During those anguished months, we anticipated that each holiday would be the time that they would be released, but the interminable nightmare continued. As each event passed, we were distressed that they continued to suffer, but we remained confident that our Father was watching over them. Although no one knew where they were hidden in the dense foliage of the tropical jungle, we knew that God had His eyes on them and was holding them securely in His hands. Somehow, in His divine providence, we were assured that He had a plan and was working in that plan to bring good. Over and over Paul quoted Rom. 8:32 —"He who did not spare his own Son, but gave him up for us all—how will he not also, along with him, graciously give us all things?" Our Father understood our pain.

Finally, over a year later, on June 7, 2002, word came to us that Martin had been killed when the soldiers attempted a rescue. Miraculously, Gracia escaped with a leg wound and was flown to safety. Although our hearts were deeply saddened by the loss of our son, in some ways it was a relief to know that he was no longer suffering. It was a comfort to know that Martin lived and died well—serving the Lord.

The months following Gracia's return have been extremely busy. It was a special joy to meet with President George W. Bush in the oval office and to see Martin's memory honored. As our lives stabilized as much as possible, we began to feel the tug on our hearts to go home to the Philippines. You see, our hearts are with the Ibaloi tribal people. Many of them grew up with our children and raced up and down the hills with Martin. We realized that many of our people are deeply saddened by Martin and Gracia's torture and his death. We came to understand that the Great Physician's best healing for all of us would come through our return. So we went back to the Philippines in November, 2002.

Well-meaning friends and neighbors have asked us how we could go back to the country where our son was murdered. We're quick to answer that tragedies happen everywhere and that most of the Filipinos are warm and loving people. While we must confess that it was hard to leave Gracia and our grandchildren, we knew that God's plan was for us to go back and finish the assignment He had given us. And that's what Martin would have wanted us to do.

More than ever, we're convinced that God allows circumstances and experiences to come into our lives to strengthen our faith. He knows just how much we can handle. Just as He held us steady as we stayed in Kansas throughout the crisis, we know that He will provide all that we need to minister to our people. God has promised to work all things for good, and we're eager to continue to be partners with His good work among the Ibaloi.

Resting on His promises, we are filled with His sustaining grace and peace—and faith enough to go back.

Editor's note: Paul suffered a mild stroke February 22, 2003, while in the Philippines. Paul and Oreta returned to Kansas in April for medical evaluation and to be with Gracia's children while she is on a book tour. Paul and Oreta plan to return to the Philippines in September.

🌿 **Oreta Burnham** *and her husband, Paul, have been missionaries in the Philippines for more than 30 years, working as teachers and church planters among the Ibaloi tribal people. In recent years they have worked to translate Old Testament scriptures into the Ibaloi language. All of their children have a close walk with the Lord—three on the mission field. Paul and Oreta reside in Benguet, Philippines.*

34 Gracia Burnham

FAITH IN THE JUNGLE

My husband, Martin, and I were held captive deep in the steamy, remote jungles of the Philippines for 376 harrowing days. Martin and I didn't know if we would survive. We were constantly shuffled from one location to another and spent countless days and nights without a roof over our heads. With guns at our backs, we were marched up steep mountains and forced to crawl on our hands and knees through the rugged undergrowth. Many times we were handcuffed to trees by our captors. For the most part we lived on bananas, coconuts, and whatever else the Abu Sayyaf gave us.

Even though our captors were brutal, the hardest thing for Martin and me was being separated from our three children. We had left them with coworkers to have a short getaway to celebrate our 18th wedding anniversary. We had promised to be gone only a week. It was agonizing to miss those precious days, weeks, and months with our children.

There were times when Martin and I had a few moments of relative quiet. We used that time to dream together about how our lives would be when we were released. Sometimes we heard helicopters whirling just above our heads, and that gave us great hope that we would be rescued. In an effort to take our minds off our grim predicament, we talked about many things—concerns for our children and our family.

We lost so much—even our freedom. But there was always one basic truth that we clung to: our faith in God. We remembered the promises of His Word. Those precious promises reminded us over and over that He knew where we were. God was watching over all of us. That faith sustained us even in the nightmarish moments when we stared death in the face.

Finally, on June 7, 2002, Filipino commandos found us and attempted to rescue us from the Abu Sayyaf abductors. I truly believed that we were going to die. Martin was fatally wounded in the shoot-out, and I was shot in the leg. The rescuers took me to a hospital for treatment, and I flew home to my children a few days later. It was a bittersweet reunion. Losing Martin has left a gaping hole in our family circle.

My children asked me if I was going to have a breakdown. I told them, "No. I had my breakdowns in the jungle."

If not for my absolute faith in God, I would have been emotionally destroyed. But I *did* have that foundation of faith, and it has sustained me.

Others ask me how I manage to appear to be so happy. My response is to tell them that my peace comes from my faith in God and the grace that He continues to give to me every day.

With all that's happened, our children and I agree that, although our faith was sorely tested, it never shattered. Our Heavenly Father continues to be with us, and He provides for us. My children and I have recently moved into a beautiful home that friends and neighbors built for us in Rose Hill, Kansas.

So even though my children and I miss Martin tremendously, our Heavenly Father continues to meet all of our needs. Our faith in Him is still rock solid, and we're counting on Him to get us through everything that comes across our path.

🕊 **Gracia Burnham** *and her husband, Martin, were missionaries in the Philippines for 17 years before they were kidnapped and held captive for more than a year. Her faith in God remains strong. Gracia is a gifted speaker and has written a book about their experiences. She and her children currently live in Rose Hill, Kansas.*

35 🖋 Brenda Campbell

IN THE HANDS OF GOD

I was born into an extremely dysfunctional family in Dodge City, Kansas. I remember wondering if God really loved me or cared what was happening in my life.

I was sexually abused by my brother when I was a very young child. That abuse still haunts me in many ways and has affected my relationships with men.

My mother was diagnosed with HIV-AIDS and cancer when I was 13 years old. She was my strongest supporter and the one I depended on, and my heart broke as she wasted away. When her medical needs were more than could be provided in Dodge City, my parents moved to Wichita.

They didn't have a place to live in Wichita, so they took up residence in a homeless shelter. On their first Sunday there, my parents walked to a church a couple of blocks away. The ushers directed them to a Sunday School class that was taught by the pastor's wife. The loving people in that class accepted my parents unconditionally and began to meet their needs immediately.

My brother and I joined them a few weeks later. I hated the shelter, and I cried myself to sleep every night. I wanted my aunt and uncle to come get me and take me home with them.

Within a few weeks, we moved into a house the church owned. We were so glad to leave the shelter, and the church right across the street from our new home became a beacon of hope for me. The unconditional love and support we received from our church family was faith in action that blessed us greatly.

Even when my mom was in the final stages of life, the pastor's wife came and took her across the street in a wheelchair to attend Bible study. My mother died in 1995, when she was just 39 years old.

During my senior year of high school, about two years after my mother's death, my father informed me that he was gay and that he had decided to "come out of the closet." He planned to move his partner into our home—my mother's home. I felt totally abandoned.

Life seemed hopeless. Mom was gone. Dad was interested only in doing his own thing, and my friends at school were encouraging me to get involved in behaviors I knew were wrong.

In my loneliness and anguish, I cried out to God. And He heard my cry. Just a few days later, Pastor Vern Haller and his wife, Eunice, called me because they were concerned about the direction my life was taking. They invited me to come live with them. It was a turning point in my life.

Although I had attended church off and on for most of my life, it was then that I knew that God loved me. For the first time in my life I began to feel safe—as though God was embracing me. I didn't know what His plans were for me, but I trusted Him.

God gave me a church family who loved me so much that they became my parents, grandparents, sisters, and brothers. I don't know where I would be today if those dear people hadn't reached out to me when they did.

Almost before I knew it, I was in the middle of my senior year of high school. I had always dreamed of going to college but had never dared to hope that it could happen. My new parents encouraged me to explore all my options, and once my life settled down, my grades improved dramatically. With their help, I applied to a Christian university in Kansas and was accepted.

I found wonderful support from faculty, staff, and students as I entered my freshman year of college. No one was more amazed than I when I completed by bachelor's degree in criminal justice in just three years.

My father attended my college graduation—the first time I

had seen him since high school graduation. I was apprehensive, but Vern and Eunice assured me that everything would be OK, so I stepped into line and walked across the platform when my name was called. On that day, as on every day, God kept me in His care.

I look back in awe at what God has done in my life. I'm still growing spiritually, and I want to share with others the wonderful things He has done for me. I have found the safest place to be is in God's hands.

🌿 **Brenda Campbell** *is a graduate of Mid-America Nazarene University. She lives in Olathe, Kansas, and is employed as a deputy for a sheriff's department in the metropolitan Kansas City area.*

Brenda Campbell

36 ✦ Lauris Lee

ANGELS BY HER BED

Val was 50 years old when I met her for the first time. My mother-in-law was temporarily hospitalized, and Val was her roommate in the tiny hospital in our hometown.

Val had been bedridden from multiple sclerosis for 20 years. She was a young mother when she was diagnosed and battled the disease bravely for many years. My heart ached when she told me how difficult it was just to hold her children when they were little. When she was only 25 years old, she entered the hospital permanently.

Val's sparkling eyes and warm spirit captivated my heart, and our friendship developed quickly. After my mother-in-law left the hospital, I felt God nudging me to continue regular visits to Val each time we returned to the area. My husband was a politician, and most of our time was spent in our nation's capital, but we returned home on the weekends. I kept my commitment to the Lord to visit Val when we were in town.

Each time I attempted to share my faith with Val, she quickly steered the conversation to other topics. I continued to tell her about our family's joys and sorrows. I told her about our blessings and answered prayers as a natural part of our conversations. She seemed pleased to hear the stories, but there was never any obvious response concerning her own relationship with God.

Val's world revolved around "talking books." So I began to search for Christian titles to give her. Still there was no response. As she deteriorated physically, I became concerned that she would die without finding the Lord.

One Wednesday night 400 miles from Val's hospital bed, I attended a rally featuring Joni Eareckson Tada, a gracious and vibrant speaker who is a quadriplegic. She spends her life sharing the gospel with a needy world. I had a great burden for Val that night as Joni talked about her tragic accident and how she came to know the Lord as a result. I prayed during most of that rally for Val. I believed that God would break through her barriers of resistance.

The following Saturday I made my usual visit to Val. Several nurses greeted me to tell me that Val had almost died on Wednesday night but had made an amazing recovery—between 7:30 and 9:00, the time I had been praying for her at the rally.

When I reached Val's bedside, her joy filled the room. She said, "I now know your God. He's real! He's in my heart, and I know I'm ready to die." She explained that on Wednesday evening she had a bad seizure and heard the nurses talking to each other saying that she wouldn't make it. As she drifted in and out of consciousness, she panicked, thinking, *I'm not ready to meet God. I must find the answer.*

Suddenly she felt the warmth of the presence of God go through her body. She called out to Jesus and asked Him to forgive her sins and received His gift of eternal life.

I was overjoyed to tell Val where I had been Wednesday night and the burden I had for her as I prayed. We rejoiced together at God's faithfulness.

Val lived for two more years. Our times together became even more precious because of our shared love for God. She was a fearless witness to her family and the hospital staff. Although she died in extreme pain, there was a wonderful expression of peace on her beautiful face. To this day I thank God for the courage He gave me to share my faith with Val and for His faithfulness in ushering her into His presence.

🌿 **Lauris Lee** *is an author and speaker. Her husband, Graeme, was a member of the New Zealand Parliament for 15 years. The Lees live in Auckland and enjoy their three daughters and four grandchildren.*

37 ❧ Ruth Maner

BIKING FOR JESUS

My cherished motorcycle was the last thing to go. It was a wine color with lots of chrome and a helmet that matched. The bike was an extension of me that represented freedom, and I must confess that I loved it. I watched as a young man rode away on it. Sold! There was no place for a motorcycle in the apartment that was my new home.

Months earlier, my husband of 23 years left me. I couldn't keep the house on my salary, so it had been sold—along with most of the furniture. It takes very little to furnish a two-room apartment. So many of the special treasures that had been acquired over a lifetime were just in the way. The books that were like precious friends to me took up too much space and were hard to move. So they went as well. It seemed as if everything that made me "me" was gone.

The story of the locusts in the Book of Joel 1:4 became my story: "What the chewing locust left, the swarming locust has eaten; what the swarming locust left, the crawling locust has eaten; and what the crawling locust left, the consuming locust has eaten" (NKJV).

What happened? We were Christians, we attended church regularly, we worked in the church, we loved each other, and we had fun together. My husband was unfaithful in the early part of our marriage, but through the support of a loving church family, we were able to hold our marriage together, and many years of happiness followed.

Then one night he told me he was tired of our lifestyle. It was Sunday, and we were on our way home from church. He said he wanted to experience all the things that he had not been able to do as a Christian. He informed me that he was changing his lifestyle in such a way that we probably would not be able to stay together. And I remember how we calmly began to make a list of our belongings—what he wanted and what I would keep.

I wish I could say that I immediately became this giant of faith, but the years ahead were extremely difficult. I was devastated. My Bible offered no comfort. In fact, I couldn't even comprehend the words that I had lived by all of my life. It seemed that God wasn't listening when I prayed, so my prayer life became nothing more than a cry of hurt.

Right away I resigned all my jobs at church. The stigma of divorce made me feel unworthy to hold any position. I was working in sales, but my self-confidence was gone. So I found a job that enabled me to hide in an office where I was not around people. I felt that everything that defined me as a person was gone—my husband, my job, my church positions, my home, and my personal belongings.

Some years earlier I had written on the flyleaf of my Bible this quote from a sermon: "The God who created you understands you." For many months that quotation was my standard for living. It was about as spiritual as I could get—knowing that God understood me. That assurance became a great source of comfort.

At some point during those dark days I delved deeper into Joel and discovered more truths as I devoured those words. The wonderful promise of Joel 2:25-26 became a thread of faith that held me steady: "I will restore to you the years that the swarming locust has eaten, the crawling locust, the consuming locust, and the chewing locust. . . . You shall eat in plenty and be satisfied, and praise the name of the LORD your God, who has dealt wondrously with you" (NKJV). Slowly I began to sense God fulfilling that promise.

I was totally surprised when one of my former pastors, a

widower, called to ask me to go out with him. Our relationship progressed, and after some time he asked to marry me. I happily agreed. We married and moved to Clarksville, Tennessee, where he became an associate pastor for a church there. It was the beginning of the restoration of the years that the locusts had eaten.

My husband, Bob, has a library full of books—far more than I ever had. The church provided a parsonage for us until we could afford to purchase our own place. One by one, God restored what had been lost. It seemed that there was no end to the good things that He was doing for me.

To my amazement, I began to feel a reinstatement of my call to Christian ministry.

Through encouragement from Bob and after much prayer, I became involved in personal soul-winning again. For more than seven years I have served our church as the evangelism pastor. It has been a joy over these years to see more than 1,000 men, women, and children give their hearts to the Lord.

I have learned and am constantly reminded that our loving Father is fair and that I can trust Him. He is with me when life is good and when life is not so good. He never seems to get in a hurry, but His timing is always just right.

I am now known as the "biker salvation lady." In our garage is parked a yellow and cream motorcycle trimmed out in black with lots of chrome, a matching helmet, and saddlebags. It's fun to ride it when I go calling on newcomers. Somehow, I don't fit the stereotypical image that many of them have of a "preacher woman."

Today, not even a swarm of locusts can keep up with me as I ride through life—biking for Jesus!

Ruth Maner *and her husband, Bob, are members of the pastoral staff of their church in Clarksville, Tennessee, where Ruth serves as evangelism pastor. She travels the country as a speaker and evangelism trainer.*

38 ❦ Jenica Baldwin

A House of Faith

I grew up in a Christian home with great parents. Plus my best friend lived in the same house—my brother, Matt.

Throughout high school and the first part of college my faith in God wasn't steady. God eventually led me into a renewed relationship with Him during my sophomore year of college. After that, I left the university I was attending and transferred to a Christian university in the Los Angeles area.

I knew only one person at my new school—my brother's friend. I struggled with loneliness, but I came to a deeper understanding of Paul's words: "'My grace is sufficient for you, for my power is made perfect in weakness.' Therefore I will boast all the more gladly about my weaknesses, so that Christ's power may rest on me. That is why, for Christ's sake, I delight in weaknesses, in insults, in hardships, in persecutions, in difficulties. For when I am weak, then I am strong" (2 Cor. 12:9-10).

A year later, our family faced the trial of my dad's cancer. Even though I was at my weakest, my faith in Christ was strong. I trusted in God's healing hand, and He blessed us by completely restoring my dad's health.

A month before college graduation I got serious about my life after college. What was God's plan for me? Where did He want me to go? I wrote in my journal, "Lord, please show me where to live, who to live with, and where to work. I want to go wherever You want me to go."

Soon I felt led to leave California. I didn't really understand why I was feeling this way, because I loved the area and many wonderful friends there. But as graduation grew closer, I decided to move back to Kansas and search for a job.

After graduation in December, my dad and I talked about what I should do and where I should live. Washington, D.C., kept coming up. A friend of our family, Todd Tiahrt, is a member of Congress, and the possibility of my interning for him on Capitol Hill was mentioned. My dad encouraged that idea, because he knew it would be a good experience that could lead to other opportunities.

Another friend of ours who works at the White House mentioned another job possibility, and even though it seemed very remote, she encouraged me to send my résumé.

I was delighted when I was offered a staff position in Congressman Tiahrt's office. Just as my mom and I were boarding the plane to Washington, D.C., to find a place for me to live and get me settled in, my cell phone rang. It was my friend who worked at the White House. She said the Office of Public Liaison wanted to interview me for an available position. I told her I was on my way to D.C. and would be there in a few hours.

During that flight I prayed continuously that God would guide me and use me where He wanted me.

When we arrived in D.C., we visited Congressman Tiahrt, toured his offices, and met the people we thought I would be working with. Then Mom and I proceeded to the White House for my interview for the internship.

I sensed an immediate rapport with the lady who interviewed me, and we talked for quite a while. She offered me an unpaid internship, and I told her I would get back with her as I had been offered another position and would need to think about it.

As I was praying about these two options, I felt torn. I wasn't thrilled about an unpaid internship—even if it was at the White House. I spoke with several people and prayed a lot. My parents encouraged me to do whatever I wanted. My dad said, "I've supported you for 22 years. What's another six months?"

Housing options in Washington, D.C., are very limited. A friend of my parents called to suggest that I live in a Christian women's dorm, although it was unlikely there would be an opening available. We decided to try anyway, and to our amazement there had just been a cancellation and they had a room I could rent for one month. The downside was that I would have a roommate. I was less than thrilled. I didn't want to live in a dorm again. And I certainly didn't want to live in a dorm with a stranger for a roommate.

I struggled with my pride: I would be working without pay and living in a dorm. My mom prayed with me and encouraged me to move into the dorm and continue looking for another place. She said maybe I would eventually find a roommate to share an apartment. She helped me as I tearfully settled in and then flew home, leaving me with a new job and an unknown roommate.

My journal shows the following entry for January 13, 2002: "My first day alone in D.C. I cannot imagine moving alone to D.C. without the hope, assurance, strength, and security I find in You. Thank You for providing me with so much, Lord." God had worked out the details that brought me to D.C., so I was confident He would take care of every aspect of my life.

And He has. My new *Christian* roommate and I hit it off immediately. She was instantly like a sister to me, and she and I moved into an apartment together after that first month. I interned for three months before the Lord provided me with a full-time position in the Office of Public Liaison—a perfect opportunity.

In these past months God has provided for my every need. I have learned to sit back in prayer and faith waiting for His next adventure.

𝕝 **Jenica Baldwin** *received her bachelor's of art degree in communications from Azusa Pacific University in Azusa, California. She currently works in Washington, D.C., in the Office of Public Liaison.*

39   Dianna Booher

IN MY DREAMS

At 2 A.M. my husband reached over to touch me and said simply, "You're here." I roused only slightly, heard him pad down the hallway toward the kitchen, and dozed back to sleep.

Later when I pulled into my parking slot at the office, I saw him through the window, waiting in my office. Although we work together in our business, we leave at different times in the morning and have different schedules for the day. As soon as I put my briefcase inside, he took me in his arms and whispered, "I'm so glad you're here."

When he finally released me, he said, "I had a terrible dream last night. I couldn't get it out of my mind. I kept waking up in a cold sweat. I tried getting up and walking around, but every time I went back to sleep, the dream just kept going. So I just got up and stayed up the rest of the night."

One look at his tired eyes and ashen face confirmed his lack of sleep.

"I dreamed that you were in a McDonald's restaurant, and there was a random shooting, and somebody called me to come identify you. And there were these bodies everywhere on the floor, covered with coats and blankets. I was frantic, yanking up the coats, hoping I wouldn't find you." His voice grew more urgent as he continued to describe the dream, and his eyes filled with tears. "And I kept running from one police officer to the next, telling them maybe you weren't there after all. I was running into the rest room and back outside to your car, trying to find you—everywhere but on that floor. It was the most horrible dream."

He squeezed me again more tightly in his arms and repeated the same words: "But you're here. I'm so glad you're here."

The dream bothered him for two days. It had been generated, we felt sure, by our late-night discussion just before falling off to sleep, centering on my younger brother, Keith, recently diagnosed with cancer.

Tolstoy wrote, "All happy families are alike; but each unhappy family is unhappy in its own way." Our happy family growing up did all the routine things happy families do. Our parents watched us play our basketball, football, and baseball games. We traveled to visit grandparents routinely to eat pumpkin pie, fried chicken, homemade bread, and goulash that had simmered for hours in anticipation of our visit. We built tree houses with our cousins. We played tag until somebody skinned a knee and had to go inside for Band-Aids. We took vacations, attended parties, and sang around campfires. We argued over who sat by the window on long trips and who caused whom to spill the Coke onto the carpet.

The routineness of a happy childhood had perhaps dulled its importance in our lives as adults.

Keith and I sat in his hospital room scratching our heads about what had happened to our connection as brother and sister. To outsiders, ours still looked like a close relationship. We talk by phone every few weeks, we gather around our parents' table for birthday and holiday meals, we exchange Christmas gifts and birthday cards, we visit in each other's homes a few times a year, and play a game of 42 now and then. We take an interest in each other's children's lives—passing around baby clothes and secondhand furniture for college apartments.

"You and I haven't really stayed in touch all these years," he said to me from the side of his hospital bed.

At first I was surprised, even hurt, at the comment. Was he saying that he couldn't feel my concern through his ordeal? How could that be? I visited. I sent cards. I phoned every day of his hospitalization. I prayed daily and told him so.

But as I watched his tears fall and felt my own trickle down

my face, I decided that he was right. We had not connected our hearts in a long time. Instead, we had been going through the family rituals, skimming along on the surface of life, without watching and bracing for the waves.

That night as we sat in the falling darkness in his hospital room facing his uncertain future, we shared our souls—our dreams, our regrets, our fears, and our pain—not as children but as adults. As we talked, I began to see anew the heart of this gentle man, my brother, as if I were seeing him for the first time.

My thoughts rolled back to the year I married and moved away from home as he left for college. When my husband and I brought our first baby home to my parents for weekend visits, Keith, still a single man of 20, swept him up into his arms and chucked his chin. As Jeff grew from a toddler to a teen and even as Keith married and had toddlers of his own, he was never too busy to take my two to get ice cream, to play catch on the nearby ball field, or to let them drive his car in preparation for earning the money for their own.

As a father of teens, he judged debate contests, fed 4-H calves, and took his turn staffing snow-cone concession stands.

As a husband, he welcomed his in-laws for extended visits, waited on his wife's elderly aunt while she recuperated from hip surgery, and took in a brother-in-law while he was going through a divorce.

As a church member, he had befriended the pastor and landscaped his yard, hosted youth parties in his swimming pool, and for years changed baby diapers and read stories in the church nursery.

In his spare time he had landscaped half his city. With his own landscape business as a moonlighting hobby, he offered his services free of charge to nonprofit groups in the neighborhood: his children's schools, the churches, the recreational centers.

In recent years, when my husband and I decided to move back to the city, he took two days off work to drive us all over the area, offering his recommendations on where to buy land and build our house. And once the builder had worked his magic and we had moved in, he took his remaining vacation week to help us put in our yard and sprinkler system.

How long had it been since I had seen my brother through these eyes?

During his fourth week of daily radiation treatments, I phoned one evening about bedtime to ask how he was feeling. My sister-in-law answered. "He's pretty tired. The doctor said these megadoses would almost wipe him out every day. And he's still trying to work six hours a day."

"If he's still awake, let me say hello to him," I said.

"Actually, he's not here. He's gone over to visit Mrs. Stephens for a few minutes," my sister-in-law explained. I recognized the name of an elderly widow who had been a friend of the family. "He put in some flower beds for her a few weeks ago, and he just wanted to check on her and see if she needed anything else."

So like him. Was this the same brother with whom I had shared daily and weekly rituals so lightly? Why had I taken his being there for me so much for granted? Why do we understand the fragility of life only when we're about to lose it?

Now in the face of grave illness, we have taken the time to discuss our lives. We have cried together, reconnected our hearts, examined our souls, and sorted out our responsibilities and plans for the future. In the grip of death, we see each other more clearly.

Sometimes God sustains and comforts us himself—as in our first hearing the traumatic news of my brother's cancer. Through prayer and our faith in Him, God gives us comfort and peace that whatever the outcome, He will sustain us through it all.

And at other times God's provision in time of trouble is our connection or reconnection with one another. Preoccupied, sick, or discouraged, we may disengage from the very source of help and hope. Just as in times of physical disaster or injury, not everyone has the strength or the will to help himself or herself. At such times, the other person's future may rest on our ability to hold on to him or her. Hold on, and then hold longer.

Rituals need to ripen into reality shared at the center of our being. As with my husband's dream, often we need the reassuring physical touch of a loved one to say, "You're here. I'm so glad you're here."

As an unknown author said, when we die we leave behind us all that we have and take with us all that we are.

Jesus said, "I am the resurrection and the life. He who believes in me will live, even though he dies; and whoever lives and believes in me will never die" (John 11:25-26).

Adapted from Dianna Booher, *Well Connected: Power Your Own Soul by Plugging into Others* (Nashville: W Publishing). Used by permission.

🖋 **Dianna Booher** *is the author of 41 books. In addition to presenting keynotes on life balance and personal productivity, her Dallas-Fort Worth firm, Booher Consultants, offers oral, written, and interpersonal communication training. She and her husband, Vernon, live in Grapevine, Texas. They have two grown children and six grandchildren.*

40  Kay Arthur

JESUS IS ALL I NEED

As long I live I will always remember July 16, 1963. That was the day I was saved. Oh, how I *needed* saving!

I had been at a party the night before where a friend named Jim had nailed me with a question. He asked, "Why don't you quit telling God what you want and tell Him that Jesus Christ is all you need?" His words angered me.

Curtly, I responded, "Jesus is not all I need." I began to list what I thought I needed, checking each one off on a finger starting with "I need a husband; I need security" on and on. When I finished numbering my needs on one hand, I decided that I had proven my point. So I turned away abruptly and headed home.

As I drove back home, I thought back over my life. I was religious and had been raised in church. We spent every Sunday in church. If anyone had asked me if I were a Christian, I would have said, "Of course, I'm a Christian! I live in America and go to church!" Our family moved a lot, and the first thing we always did was find a new church—then we looked for a house. That's how important religion was to us. I was brought up in youth groups and later thought I was a great Sunday School teacher.

When I went to church I would genuflect (because I thought I looked good doing that), slide into my pew, pull down the kneeling bench, kneel, and fold my hands because that's what's expected when you go to church. Then I looked around to see if there were any new guys in church. I had no idea what it meant to have faith in God. I had a religion but not a relationship with God.

I had a strong, strong desire to be married. As a young girl I had played with baby dolls and planned my house. We had a wonderful family, and my parents had a great marriage. I had an idealistic dream of what my life would be like. So I needed a husband.

Movies were my favorite thing. I loved them. They fed my vivid imagination, and I dreamed of love at first sight. Movies, magazines, books—all of them caused my hormones to come alive with imagination. I wanted to be loved, and men were my focus.

One of the young men who took me out was named Tom. He excelled in sports. On our first date Tom mentioned God. I thought, *This is wonderful—you're religious too.* I didn't realize then that God is easy to talk about. However, talking about Jesus Christ with affection and intimacy or even asking people if they believe in Him can be hard to do and say.

Tom was a real gentleman, looked great in a white dinner jacket, belonged to the country club, and had a nice car. Later, when he asked me to marry him, he put a huge diamond on my finger. People were so impressed with that ring, and I was impressed that they were impressed. Although his parents were somewhat difficult and drank a little too much, it seemed that I had found my dream—just like in the movies.

We had a beautiful wedding, and the church was full. I wore a dress my parents couldn't begin to afford, and we went to Bermuda for our honeymoon. But my idealistic bubble of Hollywood's version of love and romance was popped when Tom told me in Bermuda, "You are now my wife, and these are the things I don't like about you and want you to change." My dreams were shattered. It wasn't long before I discovered that Tom had a real problem with depression. I felt trapped and began to think I had made a mistake.

Tom was a genius, and after graduating from engineering school, he became a commissioned officer in the United States Navy. While I was pregnant with our first son, Tom went into flight training, but he went into another bout of depression and dropped out. From the world's perspective we had everything—but we were miserable.

I continued to feel twinges of regret about our marriage but was very excited when I got pregnant with our second son. At this point in our marriage, Tom seemed to get depressed more often. When he was discharged from the service, he decided to study for the ministry and enrolled in seminary. I thought that was wonderful. He looked so handsome in a uniform, and I knew he would look great in a clerical collar.

Tom was very controlling. Even though I was working, I had to account to him for every penny. So my unhappiness grew.

One day Tom came home and said, "I'm dropping out of seminary." So we moved away, and he went into engineering. As his depression increased, I became depressed as well. I started sleeping a lot, because in my dreams I could have what I wanted —wonderful romances and a perfect marriage. My boys would come and say, "Mother, get up. We're hungry." I would yell at them, turn over, and go back to sleep so I could dream. I felt so guilty!

Although materially we seemed to have it all, we were very unhappy. I began to model, and that was very fulfilling for me. One night when I came home, Tom and I began to argue, and I provoked him. Although it was totally out of character, he backhanded me.

I said, "Tom, it's over. I've had it!" I took off my ring and threw it at him. Our marriage had lasted only six years.

I took our two boys and moved back to Virginia into our former minister's home for a while. Finally the boys and I moved into an apartment.

One day I stood in that apartment and shook my fist at God and said, *I'll see You around town, God. I'm going to find someone to love me.* And I went out to look for someone. I went from one man to another man looking for love. I did things I'm so ashamed of. While I tried to be a good mother, I later found out that my older son was aware of my immorality.

I believed that I could find satisfaction in these worldly

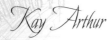

pursuits. The truth, however, was that I had been conscious for months that the way I was living was not pleasing to God.

Because of my lifestyle, it was apparent to everyone who was watching that nothing good was at work within me. There was no way to excuse my sins. Somehow Jim's words that night at the party made me realize that although I had a few "things," I was impoverished—in spirit. And I had no resistance to temptation. I tried and tried, but I could not quit sinning.

Because of failure after failure in striving to abandon my immoral ways, I finally decided that I would never be free. A deep-seated soul sickness permeated my being. Even though I was a registered nurse and was actively involved in the physical healing of those in my care, I needed a physician for my *soul*. Try as I may, there was no way for me to find healing within myself.

There were days when I would whisper deep within myself, *I wish I could be born again—that I could just start over.* During those times I fantasized about "if only" and "what might have been."

As incongruous as it might seem, even with my church background I had no real knowledge of the Bible. I couldn't remember a single person ever confronting me about my salvation. I believed that church membership and being good would earn me a ticket to heaven. As I continued in my sin and those around me continued in the same lifestyle, my definition of "good" changed as time went on. I never thought about life after death. And when it came to heaven or hell, it was simply what life turned out to be—a little bit of hell or a bit of heaven. That was it—nothing more!

But Jim's words at the party that night played over and over in my mind. When I awakened on that July 16, I called in sick to the physician's office where I worked. It wasn't a lie. I thought, *I have a sickness no one can cure, because it's not physical.* As I cared for my sons that morning, I was suddenly struck with the realization of how much they needed my love.

I ran upstairs, fell to my bedroom floor, and cried out to

God. O God, I don't care what You do to me. I don't care if I never see another man. I don't care if You paralyze me from the neck down. I don't care what You do to my two boys—these were the absolute worst things that could happen to me—if You'll just give me peace! The Great Physician, Jehovah-rapha—the Lord who heals—heard my desperate cry, and He healed my soul that day! For the first time in my life, He gave me the faith to believe that I could be well. I believed in Him, and He set me free!

Since that morning on the floor by my bed, that grain of faith has grown and multiplied. He has given me the security that I had been seeking all those years.

A Christian friend introduced me to Dave. He gave me a copy of the Phillips translation of the Bible. I devoured the Word. I was so excited about what I was reading. Dave also gave me Christian biographies to read. Seeds of truth were being dropped into my life. I continued to devour God's Word.

As Dave and I spent hours discussing the Word, I became convinced that God wanted me to marry him. But when he talked to two ministers about marrying me, they told him he couldn't because I was divorced. I was hurt and angry. I went upstairs and watched him drive away. Then I fell on my bed sobbing violently. God's words came to my heart. It was as though He asked, "Am I not adequate for everything?" Immediately, I stopped crying, blew my nose, and got off the bed.

I wanted to be a woman of God, no matter the cost. So I told God that I would go back to Tom, even though I no longer loved him. I had spoken with Tom from time to time. Several times he had told me, "I'm going to kill myself." And before I was saved I had answered, "Well, do a good job. I want your money!"

After I was saved I tried to tell Tom what had happened when I found Jesus. He told me that was fine for me but not for him. I decided to write a letter to him.

I had been in an automobile accident and was scheduled to have a cervical fusion. Before being admitted to the hospital that

Sunday afternoon, I went to church. Going to church was so different once I was saved.

When I walked into the house after church, the phone was ringing. It was my office calling to tell me I had a message to call Tom's parents. When I did, Tom's father told me. "Tom's dead. He hung himself."

Horrified, I said, "I'll be there."

Then I slid to my knees and cried out to God. I felt accountable for Tom's death. I had verbally helped him tie the rope around his neck! It was then, on my knees, that I experienced God's grace as He brought three scriptures to my mind. He gave me the strength and wisdom I needed.

When I got to Tom's home, his family had been drinking all day. I had my Bible with me. His father said, "Get that Bible out of here! Don't you know how many bricks I put into my church? I'm as good a Christian as you are!"

I went to Tom's apartment and saw the door where he had hung himself. I found a poem about God that he had cut out of a magazine. At the funeral home I looked at the swollen face and broken body of that 31-year-old man. During the service I realized that his coffin was sitting right where we had said our wedding vows. My heart broke.

Afterward I asked God what He wanted me to do. For weeks and months I prayed for Him to make it clear. Then I began to feel that He wanted me to go to Bible school. I reasoned that I could be the school nurse there, but the Bible school I applied to rejected me. Then I met a couple at a child evangelism camp. They were going to a Bible school in Tennessee, and I felt that God told me, *Go with them.* So although I had not been accepted, did not have a job, and did not have a place to live, I loaded my things into a U-Haul, and the boys and I left for Tennessee. And God did incredible things!

He miraculously enabled me to buy a house. I got a job at a local hospital. The school accepted me. Chapel was a joyous experience for me. I just stood there and wept as I heard the music and messages. I bawled my way through classes. I was like a sponge soaking up everything.

As I studied, I began asking God if He wanted me to be married again. I told Him that if He had a husband for me He would have to bring that man to me. Somehow, I began to feel that God would find a husband for me.

One day in school a friend asked me, "Do you know Jack Arthur?" He was a missionary in South America who had been stoned for his faith, and we had been praying for him. Sometime later, as I fell to my knees in a distressing moment, the Lord spoke to my heart: *You're going to marry Jack Arthur.* I didn't even know what he looked like! So I went to the missions office and got one of his prayer cards so I'd know what he looked like when he showed up.

The small hospital where I worked called one day to tell me I wasn't needed at work that night. I decided to attend a recital at school since I was free for the evening. Jack Arthur was there! I recognized him from the picture. I didn't know it at the time, but he had come home from the mission field because his grandfather was dying. After the recital I took my boys to get ice cream, and Jack was there too. We talked for a while, and he said, "I'm going back to South America in December." I thought, *You don't know it, but I'm going with you!*

He left the next morning, and I started summer school. Several weeks later as I crossed the street, there was Jack Arthur! Later he told me he had gone home to tell his mother about this widow he had met who had two sons. In November he called and asked me to marry him. I answered, "Jack, God told me 11 months ago that I was going to marry you!" God had given me a wonderful husband!

Time after time I have found God to be my all-sufficient One. He has protected me and loved me through a multitude of crises. He sustained me through the guilt that followed Tom's suicide. He enabled me to survive single parenthood when I cried out to

Him about my feelings of inadequacy as a mother. He has helped me with enormous financial needs. He has always caught me when I failed and fell flat on my face. During times of defeat, depression, failure, fear, and exhaustion, He has given me the strength to carry on. And it's all because I came to know Him through His Word! I have learned to study God's Word inductively —by digging out truth for myself and applying it.

Through it all I have learned that without faith we cannot persevere when life gets tough. Absolute faith in our Lord Jesus Christ is essential. And this comes only through knowing His Word. That's why Jack and I as well as the staff at Precept Ministries International have devoted our lives to helping others know God's Word for themselves by studying it inductively, precept upon precept.

The enemy is always waiting to invade our hearts with doubt, and he always attacks us where we're most vulnerable. But if we trust God and cling in faith to His Word, He'll see us through regardless of the mistakes of our past, the problems of today, and the seemingly bleak outlook for tomorrow. He provides for us in every way.

Jehovah-rapha, our healing Lord, is adequate for all of life's challenges. He has kept me from being imprisoned by the world and allowed me to keep my vision and not lose hope. The promises in His Word have held me steady. In faith believing, I continually cling to them, and He covers me with His love.

God has shown me time after time that Jim, my friend at the party, was right. Jesus *is* all I need. I am complete in Him.

Excerpted from *Lord, I Want to Know You,* Kay Arthur (Sisters, Oregon: Questar Publishers, Inc., 1992). Used by permission.

🦋 **Kay Arthur *is a well-known Bible teacher and author. She and her husband, Jack, are the founders of Precept Ministries, reaching hundreds of thousands of people internationally through Precept Upon Precept inductive Bible studies and the radio program "How Can I Live?" They live in Chattanooga, Tennessee.***

Kay Arthur

Be at Peace

Do not look forward to
what may happen tomorrow.
The same everlasting Father
who cares for you today
will care for you tomorrow and every day.
Either He will shield you from suffering
or He will give you unfailing strength to bear it.
Be at peace, then.
Put aside all anxious thoughts and imaginations
and say continuously,
"The Lord is my strength and shield.
My heart has trusted in Him,
He has forgiven me, and I am helped.
He is not only with me but in me,
and I am in Him."

—Francis DeSales